LEADING

to WIN

A Principal's Perspective

Andrey L. Bundley

Morals & Values Press
A Division of In the Name of Love

This book will serve as a guide for administrators who accept the charge of establishing and leading schools where students are nurtured and supported.

Cassandra W. Jones, Ed.D., Chief Academic Officer
Baltimore City Public School System

* * * * *

Dr. Bundley outlines a clear pathway from Theory to Practice.

Dr. Walter G. Amprey, Former Superintendent
of Public Instruction
Baltimore City Public Schools

* * * * *

Dr. Bundley's enthusiasm, energy and ferocious drive to make a difference in the lives of children stirs the "fire inside" as you read these pages. This is a must read for those desiring to be an effective principal.

Ellen D. Gonzales, Retired Area Executive Officer
Baltimore City Public School System

* * * * *

Andrey Bundley has a thorough understanding of what it takes to properly educate and thus positively change the lives of young people and thus all people.

Tyrone Powers, PhD., Author,
Eyes to My Soul: The Rise or Decline of a Black FBI Agent

DEDICATION

I dedicate this book to our son, Dreyan Imani Bundley, who constantly reminds us of the structure and support all children need in order to achieve their God-given potential.

For information address: Morals & Values Press, P. O. Box 29110, Baltimore, Maryland 21205.

Published by

Morals & Values Press
A Division of In the Name of Love

P. O. Box 29110
Baltimore, Maryland 21205

TABLE OF CONTENTS

ACKNOWLEDGEMENTS

The work I do as an educator and leader for oppressed students in cities throughout this nation is a labor of love. My boundless love for the students I serve is the reciprocity of love given to me by so many. It is this awesome love that takes my mind to the words of John Donne when he states: *"No man is an island entire of itself."* Thus, I have come to realize rarely do people accomplish tasks alone.

Contributions from others, whether direct or indirect, are essential to individuals finishing a pursuit. This has been exactly the case with this project. Many people have directly or indirectly helped me as I clarified and organized my thoughts. Although they are too numerous to name in totality, I must acknowledge and extend gratitude to Leslie Parker-Blyther, Jestine Brown, Ann Douglas, Constance Forte, Mischa Green of Morals & Values Press, Tajah Gross, Tyrone Powers, Deborah Quickley and Harry Tomlin. To all of you, I say thank you.

Finally, I cannot forget my magnificent wife Shelia. She encouraged me to finish this project at times when I seemed to have had flu-like symptoms of procrastination. Shelia recalled the significance of this project even when I had memory lapses. And she never allowed me to quit.

INTRODUCTION

We Are Supposed To Win

"Next in importance to freedom and justice is popular education,
without which neither freedom nor justice can be
permanently maintained."
James W. Gardner

It is clear to me that educators are warriors surrounded by many enemies. It is also clear that we have the hearts of lions and angels. We truly believe that we can change the world by educating the young. And we are right! It will take more than our noble beliefs. It will take, however, work and the creation of concrete strategies. There are thousands of other educators and millions of parents who believe in the cause. We are not alone in this battle. As my friend and colleague, Dr. Tyrone Powers, has often said, *"We're supposed to win."* Our children are supposed to win. They come to this earth by the miracle of birth, and I believe the miracle does not end there. It is, therefore, abnormal for miracles to become failures.

INTRODUCTION

This book, Leading to Win, evolved from a diary that rests deep within my mind and within my soul. I have translated my observations, lessons, feelings and reflections into what I describe as a reflection diary. I started this diary early in my life as I traveled the tough and difficult streets of Baltimore. I was a child of the ghetto, but my mind worked as it was supposed to.

> *Miracle children do not lose their abilities to see and understand the world around them. They understand oppression, depression, and depravation. They come to understand sincerity and deception.*

I recorded my childhood observations and hid them from others who might try to use my pain in their favor. I protected my soulful diary behind a veil of toughness. As I became more educated and enlightened, I decided to dedicate my life to saving other children from the pain I hid within me. I could not allow business as usual.

BEGINNINGS

Based on personal life experiences, I have a social and psychological familiarity with the urban setting that I think lends both validity and reality to the constructs and explanations in this book. I grew up in urban Black America in what many have defined as a ghetto.

I attended urban schools with other poor children. I lost my mother at an early age. I had a soldier of a sister who while parenting her own daughter had to assume the role of caregiver for my siblings and me during my mother's illness and after my mother's death. I eventually resided in five kinship care foster homes situations as a result of the Department of Social Services findings that my sister, after giving all she could, did not have the means nor the ability to effectively give care to me and my siblings while parenting her own child.

In the midst of all the other transitions happening in my life, my older brother, who served as my hero, got sentenced to ten years in prison for armed robbery. And a relationship with my father is another story. I had both observed and participated in the so-called "street culture," and I came to understand urban social Darwinism.

This most certainly is a longitudinal study. My proximity to the subjects and the years of writing of this diary allowed me the opportunity to collect and explain evidence as it occurred. Some of my diary might rightly be defined as battlefield research and journalism. Yet, I clearly understand the disadvantage of close proximity or ethnographical research. My training helped me to resist and to weed out any biases associated with such closeness and familiarity that could impact the results. I am quite confident in my observations and the action plan I have initiated as a result of the findings.

I am not naive. I clearly understand the task that I undertake will cost me career advancement opportunities. Not all those who profess interest in saving our children are sincere. I've known this for a very long time and am now capable of scanning the false prophets when they enter into my space or my children's space. I understand that education is a multi-billion dollar industry, and too many of our children are simply profit -

making tools or campaign slogans. And anyone who tries to change this becomes a threat. "Miseducation" is the norm and the goal.

For me, however, there is no greater cause than to educate my children. And all the children of the world are my children. A fire burns within me. I feel it every morning when I leave my bed and prepare to engage the students of Walbrook High School-Uniform Services Academy. I feel it when I meet and greet my assistant principals and other staff. I also feel it as I delicately lay these words on this paper.

REVOLUTIONARY SUICIDE

There is a notion that the school system will burn me out; that the long and arduous battle will leave me a bitter and distressed old man with nothing to show for my efforts. There is a notion that I will one day regret this undertaking. Many have said that I will wish that I had remained silent and accepted the usual promotions until I was rewarded for my good behavior with a lofty position in the system. I think not.

I have never asked that anything be given to me. I have earned everything that I have, and I've earned it on my terms, terms that I could live and die with. I may be bitter toward those who intentionally abuse our children. I may, in fact, be bitter toward those who ride to political success on the backs of children who have been bent over with the heavy burden of ignorance. I might be angry at the actions of those who know better but refuse to do better. All of this is a possibility. But selling out for our children's sake is a chance that I am willing to take, not for me, but for the sake of our children.

INTRODUCTION

It is my desire that when I die I am remembered as having enlisted an army of administrators, principals, teachers, staffers, parents, and future educators who believe our children are supposed to win and that education is the tool that will take them up to where they belong— nothing more and nothing less.

THE CONSTRUCTION OF A DIARY

In this diary, I have captured not only the observable behavior but the attitudes revealed through reflective conversations and discussions with students, principals, assistant principals, parents, community leaders, and politicians. As I recorded the problems, I immediately wrote solutions that I thought would adequately address the problems and concerns. Later, I revisited the solutions to ensure that they were logical and clear, as they were often written in haste. This book is essentially my diary conformed to fit the requirements for publication.

This is not a book of research paradigms culled to explain education in urban America. I think that we have enough books that lay out the research paradigms. Quite frankly we have failed to implement the research. We are theoretical experts, but we lack action. For the most part, I agree with the statement of the CEO of Intel Corporation, Craig Barrett. In a discussion on the problem with public education in the United States, Barrett noted:

> If you want to solve a problem, you define the problem, plan a solution, implement the solution, check the results, and then cycle around from the results back to

an action, then have a spiral plan to check the action.

You can't solve the problem unless you monitor it...

We have the paradigms and the solutions, yet we remain in gridlock. I felt it important to frame many of my observations, reflections, and actions in the qualitative research methods in which I have been trained. I suspect this will make some feel more comfortable with my findings and solutions. Although, I must readily admit, I do not seek comfort for anyone at this time. For it is that aching feeling of discomfort and maybe even a sprinkling of fear that will drive us to action.

This diary relies heavily on ethnography as a social science research method. I believe in this method and essentially have been using it all of my life to come to certain scientific conclusions. I believe that its effectiveness has been enhanced by my formal training in the use of other methods, which I readily employ throughout this work. The use of ethnography has allowed me to discount, and sometimes dismiss outrightly, findings by others who have chosen to study our children from a distance. Some of the *others* have looked at urban youth as some rare exotic species. Their academic work on this unique set of beings has allowed them promotions and lucrative book deals. I doubt if I should be the beneficiary of either.

An essential factor in this research process is my training as a participant observer. As principal, for the last nine years, I have daily access to people (students and adults) acting and interacting in various situations. Within these situations, I am able to observe, ask questions, reflect on observations, and verify behaviors from the actor's perspective.

INTRODUCTION

The guide questions posed in each chapter have kept me focused on the information I thought necessary to move toward action in an expeditious fashion.

FROM THE DESK OF THE PRINCIPAL

For the most part, my professional observations, actions, and reflections have been done in the Baltimore City Public School System, but I am fully convinced that the solutions and constructs can be used in other settings.

The key to the success of this book is that the readers understand that this is an action plan. It requires work; it requires an earnest effort from sincere people.

Most of the principals and other administrators who read the book will find the concepts somewhat familiar yet different. They will find the environments and activities and behaviors of our babies familiar. There is nothing new under the sun but we can do something new with what we have and what we know to change the lives of children.

OPPRESSION

I assert here that the transferability of solutions and ideas in this book are useable in many urban settings across this country because of the similarity of a particular phenomenon that touches each urban setting. This phenomenon is oppression. Presently, we need not debate the issue of whether oppression exists in America. It would be a senseless waste of time that we cannot afford to lose, and it would be a distraction that would only help to keep us in the gridlock of which Craig Barrett speaks. Clearly, numerous works have made a convincing argument for the existence of oppression in urban Black and Latino America as well as in poor white America. Oppression manifests the same symptoms consistently wherever it rears its ugly head.

Nancy Boyd-Franklin highlights the **Victim System Model** in her book *Black Families in Therapy*. She defines the model of oppression this way:

> A victim system is a circular feedback process that exhibits properties such as stability, predictability and identity that are common to all systems. This particular system threatens self-esteem and reinforces problematic responses in communities' families and individuals. The feedback works as follows: Barriers to opportunities and education limit the chance for achievement, employment, and attainment of skills. This information can in turn, lead to poverty and stressing relationships that interferes with adequate performance of family roles. Strains in family roles cause problems in individual growth and development and limit the opportunities of families to meet their own needs or organize to improve their communities. Communities limited in resources (jobs, education, housing, etc.) are unable to support families properly and the community all too often becomes itself an active disorganizing

influence, a breeder of crime and other pathology and a cause of even more powerlessness.

BERLIN WALLS

One of the major barriers to delivering action plans to those who need them has been language. I have intentionally made this work void of academic jargon so that it might be read, understood, and implemented by all.

Malcolm X encouraged those who spoke before the people to "make it plain". The Honorable Elijah Muhammad encouraged us to teach the people, not to beat the people. My former pastor and mentor, Reverend Dr. Frank Madison Reid III of Bethel A.M.E. Church in Baltimore, consistently reminded me to keep it real and give the people something that they can use, something that they can go to work with.

I did not write this book for it to simply sit on the shelves of some library or to be lauded by my colleagues and supervisors for my ability to turn thoughts into words. I truly believe that our children's lives are at stake. I am clear that most parents love their children and will join with us if they simply understand what it is that needs to be done. We cannot afford to build up walls to hinder this process.

...And the Walls Came Tumbling Down.

He who learns, teaches.

-African Proverb

Leading to Win proposes ideas and practices that will serve as solutions for many. I have learned much while leading as an urban administrator. Although I write this book as an urban school principal, the solutions and constructs in it will serve any educational leader serving in urban schools.

Because I believe that today's most effective leader is an extension of his or her past, I, therefore, felt it important to share a brief biographical sketch of my life.

In Chapter One, *Fire Inside*, I emphasize that one's desire to lead in urban America is critical to success. Urban principals must believe that their cause is a worthy one. Not all urban principals must experience what I have experienced in life, but they must believe that the difficult experiences of urban America can be overcome. I am living proof of my philosophy that all of our children are worthy of saving.

In Chapter Two, *Self-Management*, I offer suggestions to educational leaders in urban schools. The suggestions focus on the significance of self-reflection and self-management. I reveal why the leader must manage self prior to effectively managing, instructing and educating others. A foundational premise of the chapter is *know thyself*. Leaders must be clear about their mission and focused on ideas to consistently move them and those who move with them toward that end. Distractions cannot be allowed nor can leaders allow themselves to be redirected by the negative influences that educational warriors are bound to encounter. If in fact they know themselves then setbacks will bring reflection instead of defeat. Self-reflective leadership is contagious.

None of the chapters in this work is mutually exclusive. As such there must be overlap. In Chapter Three, *Crystallized Vision and*

Mission, I share the importance of the principal having vision and mission in the educational leadership process. I further expound on the importance of the vision and mission by explaining how human energy toward both is essential, and how I have fostered this energy in the leadership process. The necessity of the leader's energy becomes relevant when he or she sees the oppressive circumstances faced by children and ultimately, the leaders because the leader must address the issues and concerns that students bring to the schoolhouse. The problems that evolve from attending to oppressive circumstances can possibly drain the energy of the leader. Therefore, I discuss the need to have those who will persevere in reaching the vision and mission despite difficulties.

Human harmony is essential in the school organizational structure. Thus, in Chapter Four, *Interpersonal Relationships*, I discuss the importance of honesty and competence of the leader to both adults and students. Attached to the leader's honesty and competence is the leader's ability to inspire others, and make them believe in their abilities and competencies.

Educational theories are for naught if they do not "touch" students through adults. In Chapter Five, *Student Discipline*, I provide effective strategies used in school to discipline students. Learning cannot take place in the midst of chaos. Students must understand that the adults in the schools are in charge. They must not see the adult authority as a form of totalitarianism but as a necessary ingredient in the learning process. Students must be made to understand that discipline is for them and in their best interest.

INTRODUCTION

In Chapter Six, *School Impact Leadership,* I unfold ideas and discuss practices that can be used to positively impact the bottom line, which is student achievement. I also offer ideas relative to effective curriculum development and practices. Students need to know that their learning will have a positive impact on their lives. They need to clearly see the relationship between learning and living.

With the tried and proven premise that anything introduced to the mind, repeatedly becomes real, I learned that it was important to meet with students often to influence their thinking and inspire them toward their goals.

In Chapter Seven, *Student Convert Meetings*, I discuss topics and ideas used to affect students' thinking processes.

In Chapter Eight, *Dilemma and the Challenge*, I present real stories which urban principals and others hear, and must respond to. The life experiences students bring to the schoolhouse are sometimes poignant, and urban educators must be ready to effectively address them. These problems must be turned into situations that allow the students to become better. There are no throwaway children. This is a challenge. Urban principals must be prepared to take on these difficult challenges, or they must remove themselves permanently from the lives of urban youth. The victories will not be won by the weak, the tired, or the timid.

In Chapter Nine, *Final Thoughts,* I share ideas and reflections essential to change and growth. I leave this with the readers so they may add to the knowledge provided in this book, as this book is only a contribution to the start of a revolution in urban American education. There is much more to be said, written and most importantly, done. Our children are supposed to win.

Dr. Andrey L. Bundley

with Dr. Tyrone Powers

CHAPTER ONE

FIRE INSIDE

Where there is no struggle there is no freedom...
Power concedes nothing without demand. It never did and it never will.
Frederick Douglas

WHAT MOTIVATES YOU AS AN URBAN ADMINISTRATOR?

The answers will vary greatly. I conclude, however, that there has to be something from the inside – a passion, a fire. If there is not a passion or fire your focus or motivation to lead in urban America will not last.

While my life has not been exempt from trials and tribulations, all things related to these tribulations seem to work together. From the experiences came motivation to do what I enjoy, that is, serving as a leader/principal in Baltimore City. The collective experiences I share are those I believe have inspired me to lead as a principal. The skills I have acquired will afford me an opportunity to work in another urban environment. I must admit; I am not a cosmopolitan. Basically, I am a local boy trying to give back to students what was given to me—an opportunity and proper information.

I am convinced there is something more than just having a job that motivates the dedicated leaders in the urban environment. In this chapter, I chronicle life experiences that have brought me to this point as a leader. While my life has taken on its own course, there have been inspirational and motivational experiences that have kept me going.

I believe that dedicated leaders in urban education have categorical thoughts and feelings that inspire them to renew their spirits to serve as educators. I am a part of this group; therefore, this premise also applies to me. Thus, ideas that are portable for you the reader, will be those to which you can identify and connect because they relate to some of the categorical experiences in your life. Remember! It is perseverance through the trials and tribulations, as well as the stamina to negotiate through life's many obstacles that give one the fire inside to be an urban leader.

MAMA'S GONE

At the age of 39, the memories I have surrounding my mother's death and the thoughts I have as I became older all contribute to who I am today. As long as one remains attached to reality, the memories related to the death of a loved one will remain inescapable until he or she reaches the same final resting place. The anxiety and pain I felt from being physically separated from my mother at 13 years old are indescribable. The emotions were so complex. These emotions were even compounded when my siblings Gloria, Danny, Dorothy, and I were separated. Dorothy, my oldest sister served as the "Rock" (strongest). She was also the teenage mother of my niece, Kimberly. Although my sister wanted to keep us together, the Baltimore Social Service Agency would not allow her to because of her age and lack of resources to care for a family. Therefore, we went into kinship care, which means we lived with our relatives.

Before I turned 19 years old, I had five kinship care experiences that definitely affected my emotional stability. Seeing my way through the emotions, however, with the help of my God, family members, and friends gave me a method that taught me how to make it through difficulty. This same method has been summoned over and over. With time and maturation, elements have been added to this method that help me even today as a principal.

The clear lesson learned from my mother's death is that painful experiences can either aggravate or motivate you depending on your perception, attitude, and guidance. The aggravation I felt because of my mother's death was uncomfortable for me. At times I found myself adjusting even though my disposition did not feel right.

Thankfully, guidance from those who cared helped me to refocus. It became clear to me that I was either going to use my mother's death to motivate me to become a positive young black man, or allow the negative emotions from unhealed pain to aggravate me to the point that I would do unnecessary harm and evil to myself and those in my surroundings. Again, with guidance and love from those who cared, I became motivated to be productive. Thus, it was the love I received from my big sister, aunt, and other surrogate parents that helped me find the fire inside.

STREETS OF BALTIMORE

My reflections on my experiences growing up in the streets of West Baltimore helped me conclude that knowledge is a neutral concept. When one begins to learn, this neutrality gives way to new ideas and behaviors in the environment that serves as a messenger to the learner. The messages can be negative or positive. They can serve to enable or disable.

Deciphering the messages sent while growing up in West Baltimore was seemingly my endless struggle. This struggle subsided only when I subscribed to a standard (God) and rededicated my life to Christ at the age of 24. This idea of choosing a standard helps even now as a leader because it reminds me that I should always be striving to reach high standards as I lead. As a young man growing up, aggressive behavior was seemingly natural. It was a survival mechanism in the streets.

The energy from being aggressive is memorable and recognizable because it is an inner-body experience; so it is felt viscerally. The results of aggressive behavior are just as memorable. They were usually negative and someone was offended; those I deemed as adversaries. Later, I was taught to win people over by being prepared, for whatever the task. This strategy lives with me today as a high school principal. I constantly use positive adages to encourage myself as well as others. For example, some of the aphorisms I use are:

"Success requires no explanation and failure permits no alibis."

"Worrying is a rocking chair that never takes you

anywhere but back and forth."

"Whatever your mind can conceive and if you believe, you will achieve."

I read these adages as a teenager in Napoleon Hill's book, *"Think and Grow Rich."* I must admit, however, that my friends and I were not always motivated to do something ethical after reading these adages. Nevertheless, we were motivated. Again, it was adult guidance that eventually helped me to positively apply these adages to my life in a manner that was morally beneficial to others as well as to myself. Even now, as I lead in the capacity of administrator in the Baltimore City Public School System, I use these adages as frequently as necessary.

YOUTH DEVELOPMENT INSTITUTIONS

My mother often said, "An idle mind is the devil's workshop." As I matured, my understanding of this statement became solid. Growing up, there were three establishments: John E. Howard Recreation Center, The Youth Development Center, and The Community Sports Club, all of which were frequented by my peers and me.

In these places were structured activities that contributed to our physical, intellectual, and social/emotional development. John E. Howard Recreation Center was adjacent to the John E. Howard Elementary

School I attended. After school we would go to the recreation center, fondly known as the "rec."

My most vivid experiences at the rec were my participation in softball, football, and basketball leagues. My friends and I often practiced and played the in- season sport until the sun went down or the rec closed. I remember the jubilation when we were victorious in our competitions, and I equally remember literally crying when we were defeated. Often I wanted to re-challenge our opponents on the spot, but that challenge rarely happened.

The Community Sports Club allowed us to participate in the same sports, but only on the weekends. The emotions during our competitions were the same as those I felt at the rec. Charlie Harrison and Tyrone Gaines were my coaches at both the rec and the Community Sports Center, respectively.

They taught us about winning, not quitting, being the best, and working hard as athletes. These qualities acquired while growing up stayed with me. Even today as a Principal, the tasks before me are perceived as opponents that must be conquered. I often share with my staff and students that quitters never win and winners never quit. Thus, it is important to finish what you start. I also share with them that we must want to be the best. Our competitors are just an opportunity to focus on and compete with excellence.

The experiences at the Youth Development Center, under the Director Alyce Ebb, exposed me to cultural arts and supported me with my schoolwork. I learned to love Ms. Ebb. She was tough, but she ensured that her staff focused on young people. It was at the center that I learned how to study, and most importantly, realized I possessed leadership skills. Ms. Ebb used the influence that I had with my peers to deputize me as the youth supervisor who consequently had the responsibility of ensuring that the assigned tasks to us (youth) were in fact done. (I still have my supervisor badge 20 years later.)

Overall, the experiences I received participating in the youth development institutions have imbued me with skills and confidence that helped to stoke the fire inside of me as a principal.

OMEGA PSI PHI FRATERNITY, INC.

As an undergraduate of Coppin State University, I was not only occupied with the idea of finishing college, I often thought about joining the Omega Psi Phi Fraternity. There were several perceptions I had about the fraternity that I believed would help bring out of me those attributes I possessed. Fraternity or sorority life, in general, has a mystique that attracts many. Personally, I like to be a part of groups and organizations that contribute positively to humanity.

The guiding principles of the Omega Psi Phi Fraternity-manhood, scholarship, perseverance, and uplift were ideas that attracted me to the organization. At the age of twenty-one, I had the desire to trek on the path of becoming a man. Thus, I believed that the experience of pledging would enrich my journey toward my destination of manhood. The idea of scholarship appealed to me as well. During my freshman and sophomore years, I delved into the life of Malcolm X. Those studies augmented my desire to be scholarly. My studies took me to his autobiography, which I read numerous times.

Malcolm X was a self-taught man who learned how to learn. His process of development intrigued me. The discipline he demonstrated to become a brilliant person served as a model and motivation for me. I learned from Malcolm X's example that one's scholarship should be used purposefully. *Perseverance* is a principle of the fraternity that also beckoned me. I thought that the activities I would encounter as a "pledge" would only evoke from me those feelings and thoughts that were called forth during tragedies and hardships I had experienced earlier in my life. Perseverance as a concept became a practice that has proven useful throughout my life.

Members of the fraternity focused on self improvement through providing assistance to others. Thus, Uplift was a principle put into action that obligated fraternity members to help improve the quality of life for others. Someone once said that we usually admire in others those qualities we ourselves possess. I believe that this idea holds true for me regarding my interest in the Omega Psi Phi Fraternity. The principles I pledged to demonstrate in 1981 are those that influence my life even today as a professional. My experiences with being inducted and serving as a member of this great fraternity helped me ignite the fire inside as an administrator.

CHAPTER ONE

BETHEL CHURCH

I joined Bethel A.M.E Church (Baltimore) in 1985. At that time the pastor was Dr. John R. Bryant. I learned under Pastor Bryant's leadership that Christianity as a faith is active not passive. He taught us that Jesus was for justice. I left Bethel in 1987 to return to Penn State University to pursue my doctoral studies. I would visit Baltimore on weekends. One weekend in 1987, I visited the church. By this time a new pastor by the name of Dr. Frank M. Reid III was installed.

After completing my doctoral studies in 1990 and moved back to Baltimore from Pennsylvania, I became actively involved in the ministry at Bethel A.M.E. Church. I believe it was Pastor Reid's focus on manhood development that really attracted me to his ministry. It was also under Pastor Reid's leadership that my thoughts as an educational leader further developed. Pastor, as he was affectionately known, taught me to serve God by experiencing, fully, God's call on my life. I gained immense confidence serving on the leadership team at Bethel Church.

Every week I had new information to take to the teachers and staff. The great breadth and depth of the word preached on Sunday helped me to address issues during the week without ever using Jesus' name at the "inappropriate" time (the laws that separate the church from state are what prompt me to use the term inappropriate).

However, I must say, unequivocally, that the inappropriateness of using Jesus or acknowledging any faith lies fortunately with the states and not with those driven by their faith to do good. Overall, the experiences from my church fanned the fire inside of me to be an excellent leader; and to make God proud. I must honestly say I am striving to be God's leader everyday. I am not yet all of what I am going to be. I am still working to be who I should be. But, ultimately, thank God I'm not who I used to be. I am getting better everyday!

PENN STATE UNIVERSITY

I attended Penn State University on two occasions, once from August 1984 to December 1985, then from August 1987 to May 1990. During these time periods, I received both my masters and doctorate degrees, respectively. My experiences at Penn State University contributed to my leadership skills as well. While working on my Masters Degree, I learned about empathy: that is, seeing issues from others' perspectives. Empathy is related to compassion, which is a significant element of leadership. The training I received in the field of counseling also taught me how to listen, reflect feelings, and build rapport.

I learned that listening involves tuning in to what people feel as opposed to what they say. For example, a student who might respond in the following way to this question: "*Malik, how are you holding up?*" with tears in his eyes and trembling in his voice by saying, "*I am doing fine.*" A good listener looks beyond what is verbally stated and tunes into what is really being said, while observing the person's countenance in the process. In this case, a good listener knows Malik is not doing fine.

When I returned to Penn State for my doctoral studies, I focused on the theory of managing as a principal and the essentials of the curriculum and instruction process. These two facets of the administration process have also contributed to my leadership development. Once I became an administrator, I realized I was most effective when I first managed myself in such a way that I remained organized, and from being organized I could then hold others accountable.

This thought was different from the management theory I learned at Penn State, which basically implied the leader must/should direct or control the activities of others. The issues and responsibilities the principal must address, however, are so multiple that it would be very difficult to focus on all issues and control all the people and activities.

The ideas learned about the curriculum and instruction process helped me tremendously as I came to understand that monitoring both of these educational facets was necessary to ensure effective outcomes. Acquiring counseling skills, information about personal management, and an understanding of the curriculum process increased my confidence as a leader and further ignited the fire inside me.

GREENSPRING MIDDLE SCHOOL

My first principalship did not come without some level of trepidation as I was charged by the Area Superintendent to restore order and routines for students, in addition to creating student success in the academic process. Inasmuch as I was perhaps afraid of what I did not know...the unknown if you will, I was certain, however, that I would meet the expectations set forth by the Area Superintendent.

The first order of business then was to establish rules and routines within the school setting. The staff, subsequently, was asked to contribute by enforcing these rules and routines. I would often say to teachers that a safe and orderly learning environment was good for all of us. The acronym we used was AAC, which means *attendance, achievement,* and *climate.* The staff and I focused on restoring the climate first. Student attendance was sustained through incentives and penalties. Student achievement was a focus that involved hard and smart work on behalf of everybody connected to the school. I grew even more as a leader during my tenure at Greenspring. The direction that the school needed and the challenges involved in creating this direction essentially tested the skills I possessed.

One of the skills I possessed was my ability to motivate people – children in particular – while helping them develop character in the process. Character defines one's ability to reach his destiny using values and demonstrating behaviors that are enabling to self and others. Thus, the overarching focus for increasing student attendance and achievement, while having students act in a civil manner, was character development.

A serious test of my leadership was training adults to focus on character development. Character education is usually questioned in this way: "Whose values are being taught to the students?" I have always perceived this to be a good question, and I answer it this way. There are values and concepts we all can agree upon.

For example, the following character words were borrowed from the Hyde School, *destiny* - a place you reach by way of your unique potential; *truth* - a primary guide by which you live; *trust* - a process through which you learn to believe; *humility* - believing in something bigger than yourself; and *conscience* - a moral and right voice inside. I believe these are values most people can agree upon.

Having led the staff and students through this process at Greenspring Middle School reaffirmed my sense of confidence as a leader and further sparked the fire inside me.

WALBROOK HIGH SCHOOL U.S.A.

I stated that I was embodied with elements fear and trepidation when appointed to Greenspring Middle School as principal. When selected to serve as principal of Walbrook High School USA, however, I was not as fearful as I had arrived there with some principal experience under my belt.

Experience withstanding, I was keenly aware that there was a difference between managing a middle school versus a high school. I did not know, however, to what degree. After being the principal of Walbrook High School for two years, I was reminded that self management skills were essential if I was going to ensure that the school be run effectively by all of its leaders.

I was appointed to Walbrook High School Uniform Services Academy to ensure that four independent academies emerged. The academy programs were to provide skills to students so that they might transition smoothly to college, the work force, or job training programs in the fields of Criminal Justice, Fire and Emergency Medical Services, Maritime and Transportation, and Business and Technology.

The key to the school's success, however, is directly related to positive reinforcement provided to both students and staff. I also believe that the appropriate incentives offered to these stakeholders, in addition to their opportunities to lead in their areas of responsibility, are significant in the success of Walbrook High School Uniform Services Academy. The enormity of the high school, approximately 2000 students and 100 plus staff members, demands management skills. I can only attribute the motivation to manage in this setting to the fire inside.

BUILDING SUPERSTARS

While having a casual conversation one day with colleague, Cookie Colbert, about music and about rap artists who produced positive lyrics, she asked if I had heard Lauryn Hill's "stuff?" Cookie lent me the tape and insisted that I listen particularly to the song titled, "Superstar." As a teacher, I often had the idea of building superstar students. This thought continued even when I became an administrator. These superstars would be those who were solid academically and morally and would use these qualities to better their lives as well as the lives of those around them.

In the song there is a lyric that states, *"What you give is just what you get...every cause has an effect."* These ideas are so true when working with students. The influence teachers and leaders can have on students are memorable for both, but especially for students – particularly when the influences are positive.

Below are two of many unsolicited letters I have received from students, who of their own acknowledgement, were positively influenced by my leadership and felt it only appropriate to issue a public thank you.

December 20, 1999

Dear Dr. Bundley,

How are you? I'm doing fine. This is Sapphire Hardy, one of your former students from Greenspring Middle School. I now attend Western High School and in my English II class, we have to write a letter to someone we wish to say, "Thank you" to and I chose you. I would like to say thank you because you taught not only me but others that character counts and it really does. I always try to keep a positive attitude in and out of school. You also taught me that no matter where you come from or what you've been through, you can overcome that and be somebody. You were never phony, you kept it real. I knew if I ever needed something, I could come to you and that felt good to know. Every time I'm about to do something wrong in school, I always think about you. Then, I change my mind. You have instilled character in me and I thank you for that. I also thank you for sticking with my class till the end, even though you had plenty of other job offers. Once again, I thank you.

Much Love,
Sapphire Hardy

P. S.
I will always remember the 5 principles:
- Destiny – place we reach via our unique potential
- Humility – believing in something bigger than yourself
- Truth – a primary guide
- Conscience – the moral right voice inside
- Trust – a process through which you learn to believe

My father and Shavell, says "hi" and have a Merry Christmas.

TO: Dr. Bundley & Mr. Shaw
FROM: Terrell Jones, 8-02

You are being arrested for being the most caring Principal in the world.

You have the right to remain silent and give us all your love.

Anything you say or do will be held against you with a broken heart.

Due to the serious nature of this charge, you are facing a lifetime of us loving and caring for you for the rest of your life.

Your bail will be set at 100 years of accepting Calhoun's house love in full.

We the jury find the defendant guilty of being the most loving, caring and understanding Principal in the world.

P. S.

To: a one of a kind principal
From: the love of your life
Date: 3/7/95

A positive and engaged response from students is inevitable once the teacher or leader passionately commits to his students. Students know who is there for them. They feel the fire inside that emanates from the leader.

I have witnessed over and over again successful teachers and leaders in Baltimore. When I talk to them, passion about what they do comes forth. This passion comes from the teachers' or leaders' biocentrism and histocultural experiences. Experiences of the teacher or leader that touch them internally (psychologically and physiologically) make up the biocentrism experiences that induce passion. On the other hand, the experiences that teachers accumulate over time are histocultural. These histocultural experiences are replete with rich reference points that also help teachers or leaders induce passion.

The experiences I shared in this chapter are my biocentric and histocultural experiences. They influenced me to be the leader I am today.

* * * * * * * * * *

Nothing ever comes to one that is worth having
except as a result of hard work.
Booker T. Washington

PORTABLE CONCEPTS

- It is important to find the good in people and things you experience. A positive and optimistic attitude is crucial in doing this.

- Learning is a neutral concept. Students are learning all of the time. Adults must try to expose students to positive experiences to be learned.

- As educators, we go as far as we can in developing the minds of young people. Then we hope for the best. In some cases, our students become what we never imagined.

- A strong faith is needed to provide the leader with resilience to maintain the vision of excellence in the process of reaching it.
- There is usually something in addition to the money that motivates individuals to be leaders in the urban environment. It is usually the school children.

SELF MANAGEMENT

Aimless energy serves no targeted purpose.

Andrey L. Bundley

WHY MUST THE PRIMARY PERSON MANAGED BE ME?

During the civil rights struggle, Dr. Martin Luther King was often heard saying there would be difficult days ahead, but they would be overcome through faith and tenacity. The tasks and challenges faced by the administrators in urban public school systems are relentless and difficult, and it's going to take the same faith and tenacity that Dr. King spoke of to ensure that the obstacles standing in the way of educating children are overcome.

One day, while moving through the halls awaiting the arrival of the approximately twenty-one hundred students, I thought about the purpose of public school. I focused on the idea that the goal of the public school is to serve as an agency that educates the citizenry of a community. This goal is always challenging because the science that calculates human behavior is not an exact one. Therefore, we cannot and will not always know how students and community members in school environments will act or react.

As a school administrator, it is difficult to anticipate the ire of a parent or a student because you don't know what goes on in a person's mind. It is for this reason administrators must concede that the primary person to manage is himself or herself. In making this statement I am clearly not implying that the administrator responsible for managing a school organization of teachers should focus solely on self and leave teachers and staff members to work in a leaderless environment. I am, however, saying that the principal must do continuous self-reflection of her skills in an effort to make any necessary adjustments while guiding and supporting others in schools. Again, inasmuch as the principal cannot manage or control every action of her staff, what she can do is set expectations for her staff – through the management of herself – that demonstrate a clear vision for all to follow.

Furthermore, there are unforeseen occurrences that the principal experiences daily and often simultaneously. Principals who attempt to address or control every event will quickly drown in a sea of inefficiency and frustration. On the other hand, those principals who have done a reconnaissance of the principal's terrain could perhaps begin to surmise that it is difficult and sometimes impossible to attend to the myriad of events during a school day. Thus, the idea of self-management becomes more credible.

CHAPTER TWO

As Gordon Sullivan and Michael Harper discuss The Leader's Reconnaissance, which elaborates on the self- management concept, they state that good leaders reflect on the occurrences of the organizational environment. More specifically, they share that leaders ask three questions:

❑   What is happening?

❑   What is not happening?

❑   What can I do to influence the action?

This reflection process can serve principals well given the onslaught of issues they face daily. The following vignette is just one of a series of experiences that made me realize the need for self-management.

The events chronicled in this vignette are not unique to those that a principal might experience. In some cases, the scope of the multiple events that a principal might encounter during the course of a day is huge. The preparation to deal with these situations calls for self-management. Thus, the answer to the question: Why must the primary person managed be me? - is evident by issues that the principal must inevitably face.

A key to self management for any principal is the use of school organizational charts and annual monitoring systems. I believe a clearly delineated and aligned school organizational chart is important because it gives the principal a "picture" to share with administrators, supervisors, staff and faculty that depicts how and to whom they are accountable. Accountability measures are essential in the management process. When employees in the school are clear about who will support and monitor them, they can proceed to execute their duties and participate in achieving school goals.

VIGNETTE: SELF MANAGEMENT

I entered the building at 7:30 a.m. Upon entering my office, the secretary informs me that it is unusually cold in the building. Teachers who arrive to work early call down to the main office one by one to confirm the frigid temperature of the building once they enter their classrooms. I ask the secretary to call Engineering Services to come to address the heating problem.

At approximately 7:30 a.m., a teacher who "desperately" needed to see me arrives for our scheduled appointment. She begins to tell me that the accountability system of having teachers submit documentation is somewhat unfair to her given the manner in which she plans and executes her lessons. Her ideas and feelings are heard and addressed. The meeting then concludes.

Following this meeting, the secretary informs me that another teacher wants to speak to me just for a "second." I invite Mr. Johnson to have a seat. Upon sitting he begins to tell me about the needs of the basketball team. Before you know it the conversation is prolonged beyond a "second." I then begin to show non-verbal signs that the meeting must end by watching my clock, gathering papers, etc. This meeting eventually comes to a close. Afterwards I share with the secretary that I do not want to be interrupted for the remaining time before the students arrive.

The principal, on the other hand, is able to manage what he requires of administrators and supervisors because he has a clear "picture" of the organizational structure in front of him. Remember, the principal's goal is to impact the educational process in such a way that it improves the quality of life for students. This can only happen if the school employees, especially those (teachers and staff) who work directly with students are productive. Therefore, the school organization chart shows exactly who needs to be trained.

It is incumbent on the principal, however, to ensure that professional development for employees is designed to effectuate their practices directly related to their job responsibility. For example, department heads for content areas such as Science, Math, English, etc. must know the subject matter. They must also be able to effectively support, monitor, and evaluate teachers. In order for this to happen the principal must guide department heads through the training processes to be effective. The training process for classroom teachers and support staff, while related to accomplishing the general goals of the school, must specifically relate to the primary duties to be performed with students in the classroom.

It is also important to say here that instructors in teacher education programs can help greatly by further educating teachers to effectively work with oppressed urban students by first understanding the realities students in the urban environments encounter. The instructors' knowledge must extend beyond the theoretical and fundamental teaching of methods courses. Furthermore, an understanding about how to effectively address student behaviors that are drastically influenced by circumstances of poverty and oppression has to be included in the teacher education curriculum process.

Finally, the annual evaluation system must be aligned to the goals, objectives, and strategies in the School Improvement Plan. The principal must manage himself to ensure that administrators and supervisors help the faculty and staff see the connection between the activities they execute daily and the annual evaluation criteria. For example, if the annual evaluation has a criterion labeled Teacher Professional Responsibility, this means teachers are responsible for assisting to maintain a safe and orderly learning environment, i.e. ushering students along during class change. The principal must inform the staff and faculty that the school goal related to maintaining a safe and orderly environment is aligned with the Teacher Performance Based Evaluation System.

Self-management is not an easy task because it entails consistent self-reflection. This reflection process, however, becomes easier as the principal acquires new self-management habits. In spite of the labor involved in self-management, it is a necessity for the urban principal.

* * * * * * * * * * * *

Every worthwhile accomplishment, big or little has its stages of drudgery and triumph; a beginning, a struggle, and a victory.

Unknown

SHOULD I SEEK TO MANAGE SOMEONE ELSE OR KNOW THYSELF?

Written in the hieroglyphics above the doors of the temples in Ancient Egypt were the words "know thyself". In his book, The Community of Self, Naim Akbar writes, *"Knowing thyself is a fundamental aspect of assuming personal power and effectiveness. An essential job that cultures should perform is to teach people the knowledge of themselves."* Principals, therefore, must make it their business to constantly get to know themselves.

This "know thyself" concept rang true in my being as I reflected upon what had just happened in a recent principals' meeting. Some executives in the school system's bureaucracy stated in a meeting that a policy for suspending students would be arbitrarily changed. While it is clearly the prerogative of the executives to make such a decision, no consideration was given or input sought from principals who would be responsible for operating within the environment where the policy change would have the most drastic affect.

Inasmuch I knew the executives were distant from the realities of the schoolhouse and their decision to institute this new policy was made for political reasons, I had to prepare myself to abide by the new policy, nonetheless. In other words, I needed to manage and know thyself because, here again, something outside of my sphere of control was seeking to control me, as is the case for so many facets of the principalship. Driving to my school after the meeting, I was confident that my staff and I would weather the storm fostered by the school system's executives. I was not sure, however, what procedural shelters we were going to use.

In aspiring to be the most effective principal I can be, I am constantly reminded that the multiple roles of a principal require that different skills be brought to the leadership stage at once. And though it may be somewhat challenging, it is unequivocally necessary.

In addition to unexpected internal policy changes, principals have to contend with external familial changes such as family dislocation and dysfunction found in segments of the urban community, which also require principals to have additional skills in order to effectively educate students in school.

It is evident and to some extent understandable that many would-be principals are put off by the increasing demands of their job. To this end, in June 1999, the State Superintendent of Maryland commissioned a task force to investigate issues and suggest solutions to support principals and help them do their jobs more effectively.

The task force members recommended reducing some of the traditional tasks assigned to principals. For example, secretary and janitor evaluations, security for athletic events, and attendance at special education meetings; as I pondered how committed principals in urban schools must meet the traditional demands previously mentioned while still having some preoccupation with the new policy handed down by the school system executives, I found resolve in the fact that committed educators in Baltimore and across the country have had to do so much with so little for so long – and against the odds have done a Herculean job.

In conjunction with their administrative role, these same principals also find themselves balancing the roles of parent, teacher, preacher, confidant and therapist. One might ask, "Aren't these roles beyond those required to be a principal?" My answer to you is "yes". Thus the guide question at the beginning of this section – Should I seek to manage someone else or know thyself? – is essential for both aspiring and practicing administrators who work in the urban centers across this country.

The effectiveness of these administrators will be determined by their will and ability to perform in non-traditional roles outside the "normal" sphere of the duties and responsibilities of a principal. Early in the process of becoming an administrator in the urban school, those who aspire to do this job must ask himself or herself the single question that Asa Hilliard asked the Collective in his article entitled, *New Generation, New Challenges.* In this article Dr. Hilliard asks: "Do we have the will to educate all children?"

Hence, along with the administrator's skill is the question of the administrator's will. There is no question that the matter of *will* is as important as the matter of skill. We see all the time principals who possess great skill, but for some reason aren't able to forge the kind of success necessary to move our children to the next level of the educational process. I submit to you this is because the elements of skill and will must essentially work together to ensure the principal's success.

I further submit to you that because of the expansion of the principal's role, instructors of aspiring administrators now have the responsibility of posing two questions to the pupils who sit before them to seriously give thought to:

- ❑ Do I have the will, energy and expanded skill to serve as an urban administrator?
- ❑ Will I be able to effectively address and respond to all issues brought to the schoolhouse by both students and adults?

These two questions are important, and individuals' answers to these questions are even more important, because the roles and responsibilities particularly for the urban principal are expanding given the proliferation of drugs and the concentration of poverty in cities throughout the United States.

The true story below titled "Tameka . . . What Were You Thinking?" is another very real example of the expanding role of the urban principal.

VIGNETTE: "TAMEKA . . . WHAT ARE YOU THINKING?"

During a cool October morning I was following my regular routine that entails leaving my office, going outside toward the school's entrance for students, and moving in the direction my mind leads me.

This particular morning, I walked to the store which is approximately seventy-five yards northeast of the school's entrance. I walked into the store as usual and requested for students who attend my school to make their way into the building. Some students moved immediately, while others held up ticket stubs to indicate that they had already ordered breakfast and were waiting for their food. I then asked them to hurry along. As I walked to exit the store I met and turned away additional students attempting to enter the store to buy breakfast or socialize with their peers who either attended the school or were from other neighboring schools in proximity to ours.

This particular day, as I was directing students toward the school, I saw Tameka purchasing from one of the teenagers who loitered in proximity of the school what appeared to be a bag of marijuana. As she and the drug dealer were exchanging the money and drugs Tameka turned toward me. She was shocked and as a result dropped the bag of marijuana. As I walked over to her she just stood there. I picked up the marijuana and asked both Tameka and the drug dealer if the marijuana belonged to them; both responded "no." I then said, "It's your decision," and proceeded to walk toward the school.

Tameka yelled out to me, "Dr. Bundley, what do you want me for?" I responded by saying, "Come and find out." When Tameka came in the building we went into my office. I asked her for her parents' names. She indicated that both parents were dead and she was seventeen years old living with a twenty-year-old sister who helped her pay the rent.

I contemplated expelling Tameka who was a twelfth grader, but I concluded that would only put her in the street with no high school diploma. So, I decided to place her on a ten day suspension and a year long detention on her day off, because she worked at McDonald's to earn money to help her sister pay rent. I also scolded Tameka constantly by asking her what was on her mind. I deliberately said to her, "Tameka . . . what were you thinking about purchasing drugs across from the school?" She responded by saying, "Dr. Bundley if I knew you were coming, I would not have purchased the weed." I chuckled silently.

Finally, I asked Tameka if she had a drug problem. She said no. She was purchasing the drugs for her twenty-one year old boyfriend. Tameka came to mind before I fell asleep that same night and I prayed for her. Thankfully, Tameka graduated that spring.

As an administrator, I was clearly given procedures and regulations to follow as it pertained to responding to Tameka's situation. Following procedures strictly, however, would have put her in the streets. Therefore, I expanded the role of the principal and included the *In Loco Parentis* law and acted like a parent. Principals and administrators who work in inner cities face dilemmas like this all of the time.

The dysfunction and dislocation in many students' families force us to act in an unorthodox manner or outside the traditional role of the principal more often than not. Indeed the decisions we make are often risky, but somebody has to make them. I truly believe that those principals and administrators who make the tough decisions are the principals and administrators who move closer to knowing themselves.

* * * * * * * * * *

"There was a very cautious man who never laughed or cried.
He never risked, he never lost, he never won nor tried.
And when one day he passed away his insurance was denied,
for since he never really lived, they claimed he never died."
Denis Waitley

HOW DO I ORGANIZE MYSELF TO BE EFFECTIVE?

Here again, as I arrived back to school from another intriguing meeting that sought to challenge my management of self, I pulled into my parking space and felt confident as I strode toward the front door of the building. Once again, my self-summoned confidence welcomed the challenge to

51

overcome adversity posed by the school system's suspension policy as this is the newest policy borrowing any unforeseen changes. Yet I was as confident as ever that I would adapt, improvise, and win in the face of these changes.

Self-management is a process that is achieved through personal organization strategies, and I found that I would need to summon these strategies very soon after arriving at school from my meeting as there were many adults and students awaiting my attention with a plethora of issues.

In Stephen Covey's National Bestseller, The Seven Habits of Highly Effective People, he presents in tandem *Habits Two* and *Three.* These habits have principles that are important for administrators to understand as they organize themselves.

Habit Two, entitled *Begin with the End in Mind,* means "make certain that whatever you do on a particular day does not violate the criteria you have defined as supremely important (p.98)." Dr. Covey would say that Habit Two is the creation of what you organize yourself to do. Then there is Habit Three, which is entitled, *Put First Things First.* This is the actualization or realization of those things mentally represented.

For the last half of the day following the meeting with my boss, I thought about creating excellence in the midst of relentless adversity. I believed that Walbrook High School could be an excellent school, but I also realized the difficult days ahead because of a changing bureaucracy, non-funded initiatives, misinformed and undereducated professionals, unengaged community members, in addition to other contributing factors. Yet, I knew it was essential to find solutions in action for somebody stated that *too much analysis leads to paralysis.*

It is crucial for administrators to clearly identify the habits and behaviors they need to acquire and execute to be effective on a daily basis. Administrators are encouraged to acquire habits that contribute to effective self-management practices. They must plan their work and work their plan daily. They must be goal oriented. When administrators walk into their schools they should know that there are chores that must be done that day which were not done the day before. Then, they must have the discipline to get them done.

At the same time, however, it is also important for administrators, especially principals, to know when to scrap the plan for the day to attend to an unforeseen but important activity. Having a systematic procedure for managing daily administrative chores is essential. The following are those administrative qualities that we must manage well.

Administrators must be excellent delegators. Remember, while administrators call giving assignments delegating, the receiver of the assignment considers it dumping. This perception is changed, however, when administrators are positioned to provide assistance or support for those doing assigned tasks. Mike Krzyzewski, Duke University Basketball Coach and author of *Leading with the Heart,* states that the leader must remove the obstacles that get in the way of a person's success by creating a supportive environment.

Support can merely be something as simply as asking the staff member if all is well in what he has to do. It is, however, important for administrators to establish a plan for follow-up on tasks that are delegated. When there is follow-up, the staff is taught by example that assignments are important. Staff members also realize that the leader is not inundated by all he has to do, but is organized and expects work to get done.

The effectiveness of our follow-up behavior is increased when we write things down. Writing things down or having someone do it for you increases the likelihood that tasks will get completed. I am happy that I mastered this method. Leaving my office on this particular day to execute a written task, I encountered a group of students who indicated that they had an urgent matter about which they needed to speak to me. I moved to a convenient location to hear their concern. While it was extremely urgent for them, it was manageable for me. They spoke, I listen, I responded, they were satisfied, and I moved to complete the task for which I originally moved from my office to do.

After dealing with the group of students I was still focused because my purpose for that moment was written down. The goal of getting administrative chores done must be for the purpose of freeing yourself so that you will be able to address issues that directly impact the educational development of students.

As I reflect on the District Office administrators, e.g. superintendents and other senior level administrators, I do not think that they intentionally attempt to disable the educational process at the school level with regards to the district bureaucracy. I believe that these administrators must define, on their terms, what is important when it comes to educating students, and to do this they are often reacting to the political climate which demands them to fix the ills of the school system. And in their efforts to comply, they subsequently bombard the school with "new" innovations and changes – that on a principal's level don't appear to be the most feasible.

Now am I implying that there is nothing in need of fixing at the school level or within some school districts? No. I am well aware that there are many things that need fixing. I am, however, saying that many of the initiatives from the top down cause a distraction often times because of when and how they are presented and expected to be implemented. Again, I strongly encourage principals to be self-managers as the phenomenon of constant change is a regularity in urban education. If we aren't careful many of the changes we as principals and administrators are forced to impose can put us in a bind, yet I encourage principals and administrators to remain positive and keep the well being of your students at the center of your decisions.

Keeping the students at the center of the decisions for the principals has everything to do with moving with alacrity through daily tasks that consume valuable time. The primary two foci for principals that require support are those that engage students in learning and guide their moral and social development. I believe that principals should acquire management habits that come forth automatically in the management and leadership process.

Here, I would like to draw a distinction between managers and leaders. Managers provide technical assistance in an organization while leaders see the future and move toward it. During the Civil Rights struggle, Dr. Martin Luther King Jr. envisioned how the end would be for Blacks as he led people through the social, political and economic struggle. He was a leader. On the other hand, Harry Belafonte, Ralph Abernathy, Jesse Jackson, Joseph Lowry, and others provided technical assistance by paying attention to details and strategy. They were managers.

Fred Manske, author of *Secrets of Effective Leadership,* provides sixteen techniques that will help principals organize themselves to be effective. He states that principals can:

- Identify the areas of your job with the greatest payoff for your organization
- Develop goals for each critical success area
- Set weekly priorities to facilitate the accomplishment of goals
- Do the most important things first and never waste time on unimportant activities
- Concentrate on a few things at a time
- Establish deadlines for yourself
- Don't be a slave to your mail
- Set aside a few minutes each day to think about creative ways to improve performance of your organization
- Do not arrange or attend unnecessary meetings
- Don't let visitors steal your valuable time
- Delegate
- Support colleagues
- Trust colleagues' ability
- Make every minute count for personnel
- Shield yourself from energy losses due to worrying
- Coordinate your schedule with your secretary
- Learn to utilize small chunks ….

The urban principal's ability to organize himself, again, is essential. The principal's organizational skills or lack thereof are directly related to his administrative habits.

CHAPTER TWO

First we form habits then they form us
conquer your bad habits or they'll eventually conquer you.
Dr. Rob Gilbert

WHY IS SELF-MANAGEMENT REALLY IMPORTANT?

Self-management allows for routinized thinking and behavior. Thinking and behavior that are positive, purposeful and prudent lead principals to productivity. One might associate routines to the concept of rigidity. However, a principal's thinking can be habitually repetitive, but the observable and physical by-products can be expansive. Consequently, the principal can be effective in influencing people practices in multiple areas of the organization.

In other words, the principal's repetitive thinking and behavior affect both the depth and breadth of the school organization. Peter Senge presents the construct, mental models in both his textbook and field book entitled, The Fifth Discipline. Several psychologists explain the mental model as "semi-permanent tacit 'maps' of the world which people build up as part of their everyday reasoning processes."

The operative word here is maps. A map as we know is a flat surface consisting of representations of features of an area on the ground. Principals must have maps (reasoning processes) relative to managing and leading their schools. The area of these maps are as expansive or narrow as the principal's successful implementation of the activities, and strategies that accomplish the objectives and ultimately the goals of the School Improvement Plan [See Diagram 1].

More specifically, the principal references mental maps (ideas related to managing the school) that he has had some success implementing. In other words, the principal indulges and repeats behaviors that yield "success." The caution here is that success is relative. This is to say that a principal's focus on an expansive or narrow list of goals can be effective or ineffective.

For example, she may, year after year, focus only on those goals in the school improvement plan that she has had success in implementing. The strategies and activities that accomplish these particular goals are familiar and comfortable to the principal in the management and leadership process. However, the strategies accomplished could be a small portion of the school improvement process. Therefore, the principal's mental model needed for a total school improvement process is limited in scope.

In Diagram 1, there are three sets of highlighted goals in the school improvement process that I as an administrator focused on at different points during my tenure. Beneath each goal are strategies, which can be called thinking processes. These thinking processes distinguish ideas to which I gravitated earlier versus later during my tenure as an administrator. The gravitating behavior encompasses my Mental Models.

DIAGRAM 1.   Maps & Reasoning Processes

Principal [Early]	Principal [Late]
IMPROVED STUDENT ATTENDANCE	**IMPROVED STUDENT ATTENDANCE**
Accurate record keeping by teachers.	Encouraging teachers to build relationships with students and encourage them to come to school.
Call students homes when they are absent.	Home visits to students by the principal or designee.
Get the court system involved when appropriate.	Call students homes to inform parents of absenteeism.
	Use incentives to encourage students to come to school
	Accurate record keeping for teachers.
	Get the court system involved when appropriate.
INCREASED STUDENT ACHIEVEMENT	**INCREASED STUDENT ACHIEVEMENT**
Encourage teachers to teach their subjects.	Review the topics to be taught semester and annually.
Acknowledge student success quarterly and semester; provide reward, awards and incentives.	Establish a standard curriculum pacing grid.
Use the annual evaluation form to help determine if teachers met expectations.	Focus teachers on data that shows student academic needs that warrant attention.
	Prioritize and focus the entire staff on the academic needs of students. Take massive action to address student needs.
	Encourage teachers to motivate students' success.
	Acknowledge student success via incentives.

	Establish a monitoring grid which keeps data on the strategies implemented.
	Manage by walking around daily, giving feedback when it is warranted.
	Use the annual evaluation form to help determine if teachers met expectations.
	Acknowledge student success quarterly, and by semester; provide rewards, awards and incentives.
SAFE AND CIVIL LEARNING ENVIRONMENTS	**SAFE AND CIVIL LEARNING ENVIRONMENTS**
Set clear limits and rules and enforce them.	Set clear limits and rules and enforce them daily.
Use the Discipline Code to guide student behavior.	Visibility; move around.
	Establish a character building program that empowers students to be good citizens.
	Use the Student Discipline Code to guide student discipline.
	Give students the opportunity to participate in making the school environment safe.
	Acknowledge student success quarterly and by semester; provide rewards, awards and incentives.

Again, the information in this diagram comes from my reflections and actions at different times during my tenure as principal. While the strategies are in no specific order, they are, however, indicative of my thought processes around accomplishing success related to a specific goal. As you can see, my mental models became more detailed over time.

There are two important implications here for those training new administrators:

- Aspiring administrators must be asked to layout or describe on paper their mental models and have qualified practitioners (successful principals) discuss idealism versus realism in their thinking.

- Those training aspiring urban leaders must update the practices used to train administrators. More specifically, action/reflection sessions should take place at the school site so that aspiring administrators can have an accurate interpretation of what *is* really happening versus what they *think* is really happening.

Adding to the importance of self-management is the principal's educational philosophy. The principal's educational philosophy will serve her greatly if she has grounded in her philosophy a worldview (a comprehensive image of the universe and humanity's relation to it) that induces passion and a sense of urgency to act constructively in her province. For me, my educational philosophy is inescapable.

Returning to my office from one of the chores I established for myself, I found myself observing and thinking about the work to be done to make our school second to none. My philosophy about urban education helped me to realize our future success in the schoolhouse depended on the effective practices relative to teacher instruction, student discipline, adult preparation to guide/teach students, and adult commitment to school policies. Accurate and consistent practice of these essential concepts would help us maximize what could be done by the school personnel.

Remaining, however, would be the issues we face because of dislocated community and family structures. These structures are most difficult to address and are usually ignored for many reasons. One reason is that it is no secret that poor white children and children of color are dispensable because historically, they have not risen to expected "societal status" albeit for reasons usually outside of their control. Thus, they are not seen as positive contributing factors to society. Another reason is the lack of commitment to a collective movement and struggle strategy, although individuals know that more can be accomplished when we work together than when we work separately.

Below are the twelve attributes The Maryland State Department of Education uses to determine an individual's readiness to be a principal. Collectively, these attributes provide the foundation upon which the principal's philosophy is based:

1.) Personal Motivation

2.) Educational Values

3.) Stress Tolerance

4.) Decisiveness

5.) Range of Interest

6.) Oral Communication

7.) Judgment

8.) Organizational Ability

9.) Leadership

10.) Sensitivity

11.) Problem Analysis

12.) Written Communication

CHAPTER TWO

Of all the attributes, I believe the principal's personal motivation is
an attribute most needed. Personal motivation evolves from one's
worldview, one's drive to educate children in order to help them
contribute to humanity by becoming productive citizens.

The principal's personal motivation should convey a sense of urgency.
Stephen Covey describes urgent matters as those things requiring
immediate attention, because they act on us to the point that we can't
stand the thought of ignoring them.

I believe this was the mindset of Dr. Martin Luther King during the
civil rights struggle. In 1964, Dr. King published a book entitled, *Why
We Can't Wait*. Dr. King was pained by both the assassination of the
four little black girls in the Sixteenth Street Baptist Church, as well as
the assassination of President John F. Kennedy. He thought it was urgent
to promulgate the efficiency and potency of the non-violence resistance
strategy by pointing to the success of the civil rights demonstrations in
Birmingham, Alabama.

I believe principals in urban environments, in particular, must have the
same urgency as did Dr. King to manage and lead in school so that
students will be able to improve the quality of their lives through the
educational process.

Some might ask if principals should possess any additional skills other
than the twelve attributes mentioned previously to be effective. My
answer is a resounding "yes." As a matter of fact, many principals who
manage and lead successful schools often reflect on and begin with the
skills needed to be effective principals. They then move from the

reflection process to a place of pursuing and improving their professional development. The skills acquired during their professional development process usually fall into the twelve categories previously mentioned.

It goes without saying, however, that all twelve attributes are important for principals to possess to be effective. However, the principal's personal motivation keeps her focused and faithful to the task of educating urban children.

* * * * * * * * * *

Faithfulness is activated by the state of heart and mind in the individual that changes not. No one is wholly faithful to a cause or an object, except his ear and mind remain firm without doubt. There must be faithful people now-a-days...

Marcus Garvey

WHAT ARE THE REALITIES THAT MUST BE MANAGED IN URBAN EDUCATION?

Given the social ills related to poverty and oppression, principals in urban environments must prepare students to address some inescapable issues in order to ensure students' progress and success.

> **ISSUE #1: Principals must help move students from a disregard to a regard for education.**

One evening I was listening to a radio talk show. The topic discussed that evening was, "The effects of drugs in Baltimore City." The host of the talk show asked his guest two questions about the topic that intrigued me. The first question was, "What do you do with people [young black males] who do not want to learn anything? His second question was, "Why do people continue to take drugs when they witness first-hand the devastation that drugs bring to those around them?"

I was intrigued by the first question because the radio host seemed not to be aware that individuals cannot coexist and interact without learning. I assert here that learning is a neutral concept. During the radio show it was referenced that "many of the young brothers on the corner do not want to learn anything."

I contend that standing on the corner in and of itself is learned behavior, and while standing on the same corner these individuals are in fact learning. Now it is the case, however, that much of what they are learning is both undirected and undistilled and therefore does not lend itself to helping them become productive members of society.

The fact that learning can and does take place, even for those who are "hanging" on corners, means that change and productivity are possible. Thus the issue of helping students in urban America acquire a regard for education is doable; the students must first be taught the value of education, though.

It would be difficult for any young person regardless of ethnicity, to regard the use of education as an "upward tool" if they have not seen individuals in their environment, particularly those they relate to and respect, succeed. Although urban students' immediate surroundings, in many instances, are devoid of positive/productive role models, programmatic efforts can be conducted to expose students to those who can guide and encourage them in the educational process.

A key factor in getting students to regard education as important is getting students to believe that they can obtain goals, which for many of them, are typically way too far in the future. The question then becomes, how do we get students to remain steadfast to distant goals? The answer is, students who are able to remain focused on distant goals must maintain the confidence and belief that resources needed to achieve their goals will be available and provided.

In the solidly researched text, Beating the Odds: Raising Academically Successful African American Males, Dr. Freeman Hrabowski III, Kenneth Maton, and Geoffrey L. Greif present how African American males sustained their focus on future goals. More specifically, their parents, in many cases, mothers of these young men, supported them as they strode toward their prospective goals in the field of science and mathematics.

Support for these African American males came in the form of parents:

    1.)   Reading to their sons at an early age

    2.)   Articulating the value and necessity of education

    3.)   Helping students find a way to do homework

    4.)   Praising students' efforts frequently

    5.)   Involvement with teachers......

Some might say this information is valuable to single parents as well as parents of families trying to ensure academically successful children, but what about those other students in urban environments without much familial support? My response is, "There is hope for these students, too." First of all, a caring and committed surrogate parent can use the suggestions offered above by Dr. Hrabowski and his colleagues just as a biological parent can. Also, students who do not have support from their biological family will have to seek out and become the beneficiaries of the compensatory resources that must be programmed into their educational and community environment.

Dr. Ruby Payne provides a strong framework in supporting students in the urban environment who do not have familial support. In her book, *A Framework for Understanding Poverty*, Dr. Payne defines poverty as the "extent to which an individual does without resources." In Diagram 2, Dr. Payne goes further to outline and define resources as:

DIAGRAM 2   **The Framework**

Financial Resources	Having the money to purchase goods and services.
Emotional Resources	Being able to choose and control emotional responses, particularly to negative situations, without engaging in self-destructive behavior. This is an internal resource and shows itself through stamina, perseverance and choices.
Mental Resources	Having the mental abilities and acquired skills [reading, writing, computing] to deal with life.

Spiritual Resources	Believing in divine purpose and guidance
Physical Resources	Having physical health and mobility
Support Systems	Having friends, family and back-up resources available to access in times of need. These are external resources.
Relationships/Role Models	Having frequent access to adults who are appropriate, who are nurturing to the child, and who do not engage in self-destructive behavior.
Knowledge of Hidden Rules	Knowing the unspoken cues and habits of a group.

Principals will greatly benefit by knowing the resources stated above and programming these resources into the educational process to help students in school and in the community. The blessing and ray of hope with all the resources Dr. Payne defines is that all of them are achievable by children in poverty, particularly for many students in urban America with little familial support. As stated earlier in this chapter, we must have the *will* and *skill* to educate the urban child.

Principals must make certain that students know how to secure the seven resources listed above. Students' exposure to these resources can be done in or out of school. Students' belief and confidence in the availability of the resources are crucial to their confidence to strive to achieve.

CHAPTER TWO

> **ISSUE #2: Principals must prepare to manage the pain of students who have been physically and mentally violated.**

It is inevitable for principals to enroll into their school some students who have been subjected to abuse and neglect, either physically or mentally. It is incumbent upon the principal, therefore, to ready the personnel in the school environment to collectively prepare to address behaviors that will be demonstrated and are related to, or in some cases, a direct result of the mental and/or physical abuse students have experienced.

My experiences as a principal have taught me that the personnel in the school will be able to effectively work with students who have had painful experiences if they are both nurturing and can encourage students to have a future orientation. Dr. Garbarino in his book *Lost Boys: Why Our Sons Turn Violent and How Can We Save Them*, states that troubled boys need more than just a trip to the mall. In other words, these boys who have been violated in some way need a feeling of hope for the future because their past and present thoughts and feelings evoke pain.

Adults demonstrating care and concern for students harboring pain gain credibility with these students. This truth is sound practice and makes good sense. Included in their pain are torn trust, physical betrayal, and other emotions that sever a relationship. In addition to nurturing students in pain, school personnel must help them attain a future orientation, which fundamentally is *hope*.

> **ISSUE #3: The principal must help move students from isolation to participation in the school process.**

We often find many students in urban schools whose reading, writing, and computational skills are lacking. This skill insufficiency pushes students away from the educational engagement process to corners of isolation. The older students with skill deficiencies become, the more difficult it is to address the skill deficits because of these students' self-awareness of their failing academic circumstances and unwillingness to reveal these circumstances to their peers. These students isolate themselves either by silence or acting out. In either case, their positive participation in the educational process is close to nil.

The recovery for these students rests, to some degree, with instituting school remediation programs. Now, clearly remediation programs alone are not enough as some of the students who manifest skill deficits also have developed a gross disregard for education, and have gravitated to youthful and unproductive misbehaviors such as gangs, acting-out behavior in school, and drugs. Therefore, resources must be brought to these students if they are going to get on track academically.

Finally, there might be other issues that evoke student isolation in school. Principals must be aware of them and facilitate a healthy and effective process to deal with them.

> **ISSUE #4: The principal must get the maximum from the educational program despite adult idiosyncrasies.**

Usually the focus of urban schools non-productivity is on students and their families. However, there is another piece to this urban education puzzle, namely educators. In general, teachers who work in urban schools have been committed beyond measure. In the face of their commitment, however, many are still affected by the various issues they have had to address over time which have influenced their thinking and actions as educators.

For example, an educator who has taught in a school fraught with violence might be hesitant to participate in strategies initiated to make the school safer, for fear of her own safety. In this case, the educator's own idiosyncrasy is related to experiences in the school over time.

On the other hand, some educators have idiosyncrasies, which are a result of experiences external to the school. Concurrently, their performance as educators is affected just the same. An example, some educators are or have been drug dealers and/or users, and their performance as educators is hampered. Other examples could be cited, but the purpose here is to say to principals that the idiosyncrasies of those who work for the school must be effectively addressed and managed to ensure that students are properly educated.

> **ISSUE #5: The principal must help keep the adults and students connected to the school and focused on success.**

There are many obstacles faced by the principal, staff, students and families who have a vested interest in urban education. Often the obstacles faced are related to money that is a result of depleted tax revenues in many cities throughout the country. When funds are low, those who work within urban schools always find themselves having to scrounge for resources which would help them do an effective job.

Over time, however, even those who are committed to urban education become discouraged because of the deficit from which they always seem to be working. Therefore, it is incumbent on the principal to keep them focused on the vision. The principal must envelope himself in the process of resolving problems and issues that arise. The bottom line is he must keep his faculty and staff inspired toward the vision.

> **ISSUE #6: The principal must work to improve the reputation of the school.**

Just as the person with a good reputation is usually given the benefit of the doubt, so will a school for which people have respect because of the deeds of its employees. These individuals will be allowed to falter periodically without stakeholders waiting to say, "I told you so." It is incumbent upon the principal, therefore, to work to ensure that the school has a positive reputation. When the school has a good reputation, those who come to the school to do business bring the positive thoughts and feelings they have about the school with them.

Former students and parents, as well as current students, parents and stakeholders establish the reputation of the school. These individuals will market the selling points of the school from the experiences they obtain by interacting with the professionals in the school. Therefore, the posture of the professionals in the school must be that of a servant to the school's stakeholders.

> **ISSUE #7: The principal must work to facilitate health care for students in the school.**

When a person is preoccupied with physical ailments, his mental capacity is usually affected. Often, students in urban schools are without the proper health care. And they come to school with illnesses ranging from the common cold to HIV. It is, therefore, crucially imperative that schools have clinics to address the health issues students bring to school.

The five guide questions of this chapter centered around the principal's willingness to *feel* and *think* as an advocate for children. These two constructs are inextricably linked. Doctors still have not concluded which comes first – feeling or thinking – or if they are separate at all. In a nutshell, however, the principal controls or manages both his moods and thoughts. I think principals would benefit from my exegesis of the words of the father of Black History.

Dr. Carter G. Woodson states in *The Miseducation of the Negro:* "When you control a man's thinking you do not have to worry about his actions. You do not have to tell him not to stand here or go yonder. He will find his "proper place" and will stay in it" (p.33).

Dr. Woodson was clearly admonishing Blacks to define and interpret their realities for themselves and from their perspective. This only required critical thinking, and the critical thinking would inevitably be that which would help Blacks find their proper place and action.

In my exegesis of Dr. Carter G. Woodson's words, I would like to encourage urban principals to acquire the proper thinking and feeling about educating oppressed and impoverished children. Having the necessary will and skill puts the urban principal in his proper place to effectuate positive change in the lives of students. Once the urban principal finds his place in urban America, he stays in it, because he will know that is where he belongs.

* * * * * * * * * *

A strong man masters others. A truly wise man masters himself.
The Wisdom of the Taoists

PORTABLE CONCEPTS

o The principal has no real control over the individuals he/she supervises. Therefore, it is recommended that he/she spends quality time learning to manage his/her thoughts and feelings in order to effectively devise strategies to hold others accountable.

o The role of the principal is expanding in correlation with the proliferation of drugs and the number of students affected by the drug epidemic. Urban principals must reflect on their will and skill to handle the new responsibilities that come with being a principal, and decide if this is the job for them.

VISION AND MISSION

Where there is no vision the people will perish.
Proverbs 29:18

There are costs and risks to a program of action,
but they are far less than the long-range
risks and costs of comfortable inaction.
John F. Kennedy

WHY IS THE VISION AND MISSION IMPORTANT IN THE EDUCATIONAL PROCESS?

Leaving Superintendent Walter Amprey's office, I was ecstatic after being appointed principal of a new character education school. The school would be established by me and consultants from Hyde School Inc. from Bath Maine over a five month period. Part of the agreement between the Superintendent and me was that I would maintain my duties as assistant principal at Harlem Park Middle School where it was my responsibility to lead three hundred students in a specified unit of the school. The total student population of the school was fifteen hundred. The principal set the vision and mission for the entire school.

Thus, the charge I had before me was to keep the agreement I made with the superintendent. In my mind, the first and most important order of business was to establish a vision and mission for the new school. I was directed to spend five days in Bath Maine at the Hyde School with the consultants hired by the superintendent to craft both the vision and mission for the new character school. During this workweek, I participated in several dialogues, reflections, and observation sessions with staff and students of the Hyde School.

During one of our sessions, we discussed how sometimes a vision and a mission are merely terms used synonymously by leaders in many organizations – schools included. In some cases, the vision and mission are no more than words on published documents that are referenced when it is expedient.

In my thinking, the vision and mission are essentially different but inextricably linked. I believe that there must be something in the principal that keeps him focused on the future of the school. This future focusing is called vision. During this focusing process, the principal envisions how things will be.

The mission, on the other hand, entails daily activities and events programmed by the principal and leadership team and accomplished in route to the vision—by the staff, faculty, parents and students in the school.

James Belasco and Ralph Stayer in their book, *Flight of the Buffalo*, state that the vision is the beginning point of a journey. During the journey activities designed to reach the vision are done daily, weekly, monthly, annually, etc. The activities are made clear so that those responsible for executing the mission will accurately move toward the right direction, at designated and specific times.

The clarity of the vision also helps school stakeholders to align the mission with the vision. For example, if it is the case that the school's vision entails students being able to: 1) use technology effectively, 2) write a twenty-five page research paper, 3) demonstrate understanding of calculus, geometry and other advanced mathematics, and 4) demonstrate moral character; those creating the mission would essentially establish daily activities that will help students accomplish the ideas embedded in the vision.

For example, students' utilization of technology would be programmed into their academic schedule. Progressive activities that lead to students' completion of a twenty-five page paper will also be in their academic curriculum. Additionally, both high level mathematics and character education units would be implemented in the academic program. Student success with these "daily missions" helps to move the school toward the school's vision.

Finally, the school's vision should be expansive enough to accommodate the personal visions of both students and adults. Generally, people are more motivated to participate in an organization's purpose when they see a personal benefit for themselves. When a school's vision has room for adults and students to see themselves accomplishing their personal vision together, all school stakeholders can establish a shared vision and become more willing to participate in the overall mission.

During the fall of 1999 after having been principal for six years, my staff and I received communication from the district office that our school would have ten science rooms renovated. We were told that the renovations would begin during the summer of June, 2000 and would not be completed until January, 2001. This meant that we would be without 10 classrooms from August through December of the fall semester.

Immediately, my staff began to demonstrate foresight to address this problem. The Operations Officer planned to move and store science equipment. Some teachers were required to float from room to room to meet and teach students. Thus, portable chalkboards and roller carts were purchased for them in order that they might properly teach their students.

In addition to these changes, many other arrangements were made in preparation for the science renovations. My staff and I diligently prepared to address the obvious particulars related to the science renovations and in doing so we were demonstrating what we believed to be great foresight. We even went so far as to think about, and decided not to float teachers who were brand new to the field of education out of concern that it would be a bit much for a novice.

With all our planning and foresight, however, we still encountered some problems that were not obvious to us. Despite the diligence of our preparing, we still missed some things. For example, we did not consider that seasoned teachers would resist giving up their rooms to new teachers – even for the good of school order and stability. We also did not anticipate students with upper respiratory problems getting sick from dust, though the rooms being renovated were structurally contained. Finally, we did not consider the security breach brought on by having the workers who were renovating the rooms leaving the doors unsecured, which made the building vulnerable to outsiders who wanted to enter. Overall, we did not have enough insight, which as stated earlier is the ability to discern that which is not obvious.

Managing unforeseen issues bode as an extremely significant quality for leaders per my colleague from Bath Maine perspective. I concur with his perspective. I will go a step further, though, and say that leaders must ensure they are not stifled too long if they come up against unforeseen obstacles in the organization.

During my first night stay in Bath Maine, the consultants and I had a late night discussion about how to establish an effective vision for the new school. I focused my mind on a concept I read called *visioneering*. Visioneering, as I recall, is enlisting staff and faculty members to engage in understanding the essence of the vision while participating in activities that promote progress towards it.

It was proposed by one of my colleagues that, "principals should realize staff and faculty members will be energized to help achieve the school's vision if they have a vested interest in the school." I agreed. Thus, I believe it is important for principals to inquire about and listen to educators' personal visions in order to effectively engage them in the school's vision.

Clarity of the school's vision can be determined by the "ease" with which the principal and staff are able to backward map activities from the future to the present. A clear vision allows the stakeholders in the school to accurately align the mission with the vision using timely strategies and activities to accomplish designated goals. The vision has its place in reference to the mission, but the key to accomplishing established goals is the will of all stakeholders involved in the educational process.

Well into our late night session, one of my colleagues interjected and stated, "If the mission ever exceeds the vision, the direction and progress of the school is in jeopardy." I asked him to elaborate on his statement. My understanding of his response is that the vision and mission should be essentially tied together as inextricable elements to be productive; just as light and power are necessary to each other to accomplish certain tasks.

In a school house, the vision is the headlights of a vehicle that guides the school while the engine of the vehicle is the committed stakeholders who daily power the mission on its journey to the future. Yes, as you can imagine, the company of a physicist and two educators with varying experiences as teachers made for deep conversation some times during the late nights in Bath, Maine.

* * * * * * * * * *

The thing happens that you really believe in;
and the belief in a thing makes it happen.
Andrey L. Bundley

HOW DO YOU GET HUMAN ENERGY TOWARD THE MISSION AND VISION?

One afternoon sitting while in the dining hall of the Hyde School during my visit to Maine, the question was asked, "How much should a school be managed like a business?" Answers varied by those who either at one time contemplated the subject, or had an opinion about it.

I was one of those who had thought about the question. I began to discuss how businesses are able to get customers to come back if they offer goods or products in which customers believe. Principals, similarly, can get their customers (students, parents, businesses, teachers, the school system, etc.) to believe in the school and its processes by having a vision that inspires and a mission that accomplishes incremental success.

The principal must always be positioned to inspire individuals toward the school's vision. He is able to do this by always knowing which stakeholder is mounting to be the customer at any given time. Not being blind-sided by the stakeholders' momentum; the principal can focus on inspiring students, staff, and faculty members toward the vision.

An inspiring vision and a progressive mission gives the principal an opportunity to focus and facilitate strategies and activities that move the school in the right direction. I believe principals maintain a focus on the vision and mission by being able to reference a paradigm that reflects and describes the affects stakeholders have related to accomplishing the mission and vision. The Business Paradigm below [Diagram 3] is what steadied my focused during this process. Again, this Business Paradigm helped me to maintain a handle on the internal and external influences of the school's mission and vision.

Other frameworks or paradigms may help other administrators. Additionally, my clear understanding of the factors influencing the behavior of the stakeholders of the school helps me to manage and maintain the proper relationship with the stakeholders and subsequently keep them motivated toward the mission and vision of the school.

DIAGRAM 3   Business Paradigm

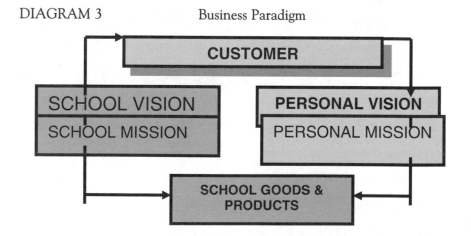

The diagram above depicts the customer having both a mission and vision that contributes to the school's goods and products. In the administrative process, the customer, the goods and products interchange between students, teachers, parents, local businesses, and the school system. In other words, the *customer* could be a *parent* and an *effective student* could be a product. Or the *student* could be the *customer* and a *proud parent* could be the *product.* The mission and vision of the customer are usually related to desired goods and products.

I always try to remain mindful of who is the customer at any given time during the administrative process. Once I establish who the customer is, I am able to determine the goods and products they desire. For example, parents who are in the position of customer want the school to help educate their child. A student in the position of the customer wants the school to help her acquire skills. Here we see figuratively and realistically how customers always have a mission and vision which directs them toward obtaining related goods and products.

Always understanding who the customer is allows me to stay focused on the vision for the school in spite of competing interests - both internal and external. In some cases, I found myself talking to students seeking a future for themselves in the absence of supportive parents. Conversely, I have observed many students disengaged from the educational process . . . for a variety of reasons. I have also, however, experienced parents who try their best to encourage their disengaged children to become customers in the educational process.

In Diagram 4 below, I've outlined the changing roles stakeholders have relative to influencing the educational and administrative process of the school:

DIAGRAM 4   Stakeholders' Roles

GOODS & PRODUCTS	CUSTOMERS & STAKEHOLDERS
Students skilled in generating educational and career options.	Parents and Businesses
Academic skills competitive for the workplace and continued education in higher institutes of learning.	Students
Professional development to integrate innovations in teaching, curricula design and current course topics.	Teachers, School Administrators, Businesses
Professional Respect	Teachers, School Administrators
Effective Teaching	Teachers, School Administrators, Parents, Students

Remember, customers (in whatever capacity they come) have an interest in the school. They typically come armed with a mission and vision related to the goods and products that they are trying to secure. The principal is responsible for keeping the overall mission and vision of the school before the stakeholders as he inspires them to execute the mission in pursuit of the vision.

In the midst of issues, complaints, and concerns by stakeholders, principals still must maintain a focus on initiatives that move the staff, faculty, and constituents toward the vision. Therefore, it is essential that the principal know what customer is making demands for a specific product. This paradigm, again, helps me to stay focused as a principal so that I can then continue to encourage individuals toward the vision.

Finally, there are other strategies principals can use to engage stakeholders in accomplishing the mission and vision. James Belasco, author of *Teaching the Elephant to Dance,* encourages principals to:

- use drama to motivate stakeholders
- live the vision in front of the stakeholders
- compulsively communicate the vision
- monitor progress toward the mission and vision
- grow people to embrace, accomplish, and advance the vision

DRAMA

Tuning in on the vernacular of the teenage students whom I serve as principal, I often hear them accusing each other of having too much drama. In other words, the claim is made peer to peer that one is exaggerating an incident. In the schoolhouse, the principal defines and uses drama as an unexpected event that calls for the faculty, staff, and students' attention to the vision. The following is a scenario that explains how we used drama to engage staff to the school's vision.

The State Board of Education used test scores to determine "failing schools." As usual, we worked hard to improve our students' scores and were confident that we would not be declared a "failed school." To this end, we planned a party one year – in advance – to celebrate our anticipated success. Proud of what they were about to accomplish, I arranged a pre-party repast for the teachers. At one of my faculty meetings, I gave staff two tickets to enter the catering establishment that would host the big party. The party was a year away.

Not only did we use drama to engage staff toward the school's vision, we also used drama to empower students toward the vision. One of the things I do as principal is convene grade level meetings (9th –12th) with my students every three weeks. The agenda for the meetings is always announced in advance.

During one particular week of the grade level meetings, I received good news from the district that we were making progress toward being named "a successful school," pursuant to the State of Maryland standards. I changed the agenda of this particular meeting with the students. Instead of attending to the items on the originally planned agenda, I scrapped it and commenced a fifteen-minute praise session wherein we told students that they were primarily responsible for the success the school was making. They did not expect our comments, and they were beaming with confidence as they applauded themselves. These students, through drama, were being subtly enveloped in the vision.

CAPTURING THE VISION

Living the vision is also essential for every principal. I must be transparent at this point and acknowledge that I am a hyper-principal with enough control not to transgress ethical boundaries within the school organization. However, this behavior, I realize, must be quelled to a level that enables others in the leadership process to stay focused on established activities and strategies of the school. Thus, I have focused on this behavior in my Individualized Development Plan [IDP]. I must fix my behavior if I expect others to change.

I realize that staff, faculty, and students profile me in their minds. They watch the moves I make and listen intensely to the comments I say. As I consistently live the vision, staff, faculty, and students form impressions of me that later become memories. Therefore, I must live the vision in a way that moves individuals toward it. Contradictions in my behavior as the school leader must be minimal. Having no contradictions in my behavior as school leader is always my goal.

I believe that principals must have within them the "stuff" (vision, focus, energy, honesty, etc.) that makes them effective. For the most part, the principal cannot stage certain actions. We must think on our feet and move with confidence. While in Bath Maine, I had an opportunity to observe the Headmaster attend to student affairs while he effectively addressed administrative tasks and teacher business. He seemed to come alive while interacting with students and they responded in kind.

I learned at that moment it is important to influence individuals' thinking in order to move them forward. Thus, moving people toward the vision is a primary strategy in any good school organization seeking efficiency. Ultimately, a pleasing outcome for a principal is to observe positive behavior of students because their thinking has been influenced. This is a true indicator that the vision is in sight and has taken root.

COMPULSIVELY COMMUNICATE THE VISION

Psychologists will affirm that any idea introduced repeatedly, takes root and influences one's thinking. As principal, I must create opportunities to communicate the vision. The vision is a mantra. Wherever I go and whomever I'm with, the vision is stated. I am able to determine if I am compulsively communicating the vision by the reactions and responses of those in the school.

My students often say to me, "Dr. Bundley, you're always preaching." I find the adults saying, "I know Dr. Bundley," and then they go on to attempt to complete the statement that I am about to make, because they think they know what I will say. Again, compulsively communicating the vision can only help the principal envelop others in the visioneering process.

As individual school stakeholders exhibit their commitment to the vision, the principal should simultaneously monitor progress toward it. Remember, the mission is daily, weekly and monthly activities that are aligned to reach the vision. Thus, the principal can check to see if his compulsive communication of the vision is paying off. Charting key behaviors can do this. Collectively, the staff can decide which behaviors are essential to reach the vision.

Faculty meetings and staff meetings are an excellent place to discuss how the faculty and staff are making progress toward the vision. Students, like staff, are an essential part of the process of reaching the vision. Although more indirect than direct, students are a part of the behavior charting process of reaching the vision. In summary, the vision for the school serves no purpose unless it becomes contagious between those who have a vested interest.

* * * * * * * * * *

When the people caught the vision they said,
"Let us rise up and rebuild."
Frank M. Reid, III

MONITOR THE VISION

HOW DO YOU ENSURE THE RELEVANCY OF THE VISION FOR POOR AND UNDERPRIVILEGED CHILDREN?

I believe that principals who are establishing and leading the vision for urban schools should start from the conceptual framework that the students in his or her school are oppressed but not hopeless. The idea of oppression must not be overlooked by the principal because of the ramifications of its affect, particularly on those who are striving to promote student excellence in the midst of poverty. Poverty, as Ruby Payne states is the degree to which individuals go without resources.

Oppression, on the other hand, is unjust power and authority imposed on individuals. Paula Friere, author of *The Pedagogy of the Oppressed* states "the oppressed yearn for freedom, and justice to recover their lost humanity." I believe that oppression is a society that provides students in urban settings "one" dollar for their education while giving their peers in another school district ten miles away, disproportionately, "two" dollars. Usually, this inequitable distribution of funds occurs over an extended period of time. Oppression is also deteriorating school buildings and substandard equipment – all in the midst of the oppressors merely lamenting the conditions.

Some students might ask, "If urban students are subjected to oppression, who's doing the oppressing?" I submit to you that the oppressor is any individual, any collective group of individuals(s), or any institution that participates, directly or indirectly, in perpetuating the injustices mentioned above. One of the most pronounced ramifications of oppression is the leveraging of power. Usually, the idea of quid pro quo is in the vicinity where power is being leveraged.

In the urban education arena, power brokers provide money to the district in exchange for control or governance of educational policies. In most cases, policies made at the state level usually do not have a positive impact or correct the ramifications from oppression. But the same policies dictate changes at the school for principals, teachers, and ultimately students. Therefore, I believe that it is imperative for the urban principal to create a vision for the students in his school that is relevant to the community's realities so that the inevitable policy changes that come from state and district power brokers will not affect the flow of success toward educational excellence.

A clear and relevant vision for the principal helps him gauge the importance of "new" innovations designed to help students while guarding educational stability for them. During one of our evening pontification sessions in Maine, my colleagues and I discussed how the urban school situation is approaching third world status. I retorted "Yes! The Harriet Tubman mentality is necessary – Internal Locus of Control – by the people to persevere."

I went on to say that I also believe the primary strategy of community education and empowerment is being ignored. Paul, my colleague, asked me why I thought this was the case. I responded by sharing that I felt piece meal strategies are being suggested and used to correct oppressive circumstances as opposed to the collective strategy used in the sixties. John, another colleague, asked me to further explain what I meant.

I further explained by sharing that oppression, i.e. Jim Crowism was a factor for all Black people and ultimately white people to distract both racial groups from a collective strategy to improve the quality of life for both groups. Therefore, those with courage initiated the strategy to change the circumstances, others who were afraid shrunk from actions. Additionally, I stated that Blacks and poor whites have made some strides and some believe these small gains separate our issues from one another. Still, there is no collective struggle. Actually, individuals take actions only if it seems to be politically correct. In closing, I shared that political correctness does have its place, but it must not supersede obvious issues that warrant common sense and collective struggle.

As urban principals we must set our minds on consistent practices for our students regardless of political or academic fads. Ron Edmonds, the progenitor of the *Effective Schools Research* stated that urban students, regardless of new curriculum initiatives, should have basic reading, writing, and math courses. I contend that given the skill level at which many of our children in urban schools come to school, Mr. Edmonds' statement is valid. Urban principals who openly adopt every new program and process reveal their non-strategic thinking which unfortunately relinquishes students' education and guidance to a process not necessarily beneficial to their academic and social development.

To avoid such a practice, principals must know the essence of new curriculum initiatives imposed upon students, decipher what in the initiatives might serve as obstacles to students' success relative the school's vision, and facilitate processes that will inform students how to effectively negotiate through the obstacles.

New curriculum initiatives and policies mean little or nothing to oppressed students, even when they are attached to graduation requirements. Many students have to be taught and shown the importance of education. They have acquired the belief that this education will not improve the quality of life as they know it. Some students rise to the occasion to meet stipulations set by the district.

Many don't engage the process immediately, but they do so gradually. Often, when they accomplish the task foisted on them, it has little or no meaning to many of them afterwards because the "accomplishments" don't immediately and positively affect their daily living circumstances.

I would like to insert here that principals in urban environments would perhaps muster more confidence if district leaders assured us that they "really" want students to learn before being promoted to the next grade. In many cities across the country, the desire for real student achievement does not exist. How else could the massive student failure rate be justified? Remember, these students are God's gifts and highly capable of learning. The dedication to student achievement is greatly impaired because of the established funding structure and politics of control.

More specifically, most cities get funding from the state and federal government often with imposed directions as to how the money can be spent. The remaining dollars come from the tax revenues generated in the city. Money coming from the city's coffers is usually miniscule and inadequate, yet it also comes with a list of edicts from the school district usually cloaked in the name of accountability. I refer to them as mere edicts because they do not substantively include individual policy designed to improve the schools, let alone the school district.

Poverty for too many students disables their school progress in various ways. I experienced poverty as a child, and as a result I understand its impact on the children I serve. The obstacles created by poverty require solutions beyond control of school officials exclusively. Yet, the exclusion of agencies, many parents and students themselves prevent progress from being made toward the school's vision. Obstacles in general impede students' arrival time to a point of their educational destination.

After close examination of curricula policy in many urban school districts, I noticed that academic standards are generally established as a destination where students are to arrive, but there seems to be no sense of urgency and no concern about making the drastic changes to address academic failure (the obstacles impeding arrival) of students.

I believe all school districts must have standards. But, leaders must concede that all students will arrive at the standards at different times. Still, somebody has to stand up and say we will accept only real student progress and achievement of academic standards. While many students in urban environments will achieve on par with their peers in more affluent school districts, the arrival of a significant number of other students will be delayed due to the obstacles caused by poverty. These students, however, must not be labeled or punished given their delayed arrival to the finish line. Yet, they must be made to finish, and they must be applauded upon finishing by school faculty, administration and district leaders alike.

Finally, the principal is the "gatekeeper" who ensures that every adult that enters the schoolhouse has a desire to engage the vision of the school, and strategically participate in those activities that are relevant to liberate oppressed children. Everybody calls with a program to help "those poor children." Principals will find in fact themselves distracted if they attempt to answer and oblige *everyone's* call to help!

CHAPTER THREE

The oppressor never voluntarily gives freedom;
it must be demanded by the oppressed.
Dr. Martin Luther King

HOW DO YOU IDENTIFY THE DREYANS OF THE NEW MISSION AND VISION?

On July 12, 1995 at approximately 4:49 p.m., my son Dreyan Imani Bundley was born. When I was a young boy, I was called Dreyan. My friends and I would reverse the syllables in each other's name and pronounce it in that way. Hence, my name – Andrey – was pronounced Dreyan. When my wife Shelia was carrying Dreyan during the first trimester, we discussed what we would name our child. We wanted our child to share our name in some way. I told Shelia about how we reversed our names when I was a boy. Thus, we decided that if the baby were a boy, we would name him Dreyan and if the baby were a girl, her name would be Liashel. Dreyan was born, and all we had to do is give his name a meaning.

By now you're probably asking yourself what does a child's name have to do with this guide question. Well, in giving Dreyan's name a meaning, I thought about my life. I thought about the obstacles I have had to negotiate with the guidance of Jesus and others whom he sent to help me. Like many I'm sure, I have had a trying, but wonderful life. I would not trade my life and all its experiences for anything. My God has helped me turn my pain into power. Now, it's up to me to leave a legacy. I pray that Dreyan is a conveyor of the legacy toward its completion. Thus, the meaning of Dreyan is, *"He who will finish."*

This notion of finishing or completion was one John was preoccupied with as he discussed the short tenure of many teachers and principals in too many urban schools. He concluded that the effect on student academics had to be detrimental.

As I reflected on my last evening in Bath, Maine, I thought about how John and I agreed that visions for schools are not always fully realized because the leadership within the schools change. I told John that I was impressed with how the traditions at the Hyde School had been sustained. We talked about how teachers and staff stayed in their positions for an extended period. We also discussed how the staff became a special kind of family. John and I agreed during our conversation that it is indeed easier to stay focused and move toward the vision if you have staff with a vested interested in the school.

As a leader in a school organization, I often ask myself these questions:

- Who will advance the vision for this school
  when I'm gone?
- Who will finish what has begun?
- Who will continue to care?

For me as well as other principals, it is very difficult to walk away from a school – particularly one in which you have greatly invested to ensure its success. Nevertheless, when it is time to move on from a school, it's time. For me as a principal, I have found a way to psychologically adjust to the inevitable departure from a school. This adjustment happens by identifying the Dreyans that exist. Those stakeholders who can and will advance the school's mission and vision. The finishers.

After identifying "who," the question then moves from who to "how." How is this done? How are the mission and vision advanced during the transitioning of a school leader? I submit that there are three actions that must be taken by the principal to ensure the mission and vision are advanced when he departs.

First, one must identify and positively reinforce teachers and staff members who demonstrate behaviors that contribute to accomplishing the mission and vision. I have done this by creating a committee of teachers, staff, and administrators. This committee identifies and awards colleagues who demonstrate exceptional behavior as professionals.

Second, department chairs and directors of programs must be encouraged and monitored by the principal to create solid thinking, activities, behaviors, leadership qualities, and purpose regarding improving the curriculum and instruction process. These mid-level supervisors are the primary sustainers of the mission and vision particularly as it relates to curriculum and instruction.

It is important to note here that the management functions of the school done by administrators are still essential for the school's success. Yet, what happens in classrooms between teachers and students is of paramount importance. The practices of middle line supervisors are the engine that moves the school organization. When an organization is moving efficiently and proficiently, even the new leader is hesitant to change practices for fear of fouling up that which is working.

Finally, the principal must model and explain "leadership laws" to middle line supervisors and positively reinforce the leadership behavior of those who demonstrate skills that they can in fact advance the mission and vision of the school. Usually, when principals leave, urban schools falter. This happens because there is no capacity built in the practices of middle line supervisors. Also, some new principals assert personality over principles, and as a result change practices merely because they are the "principal."

Remember, practices at this level are like an engine that drives the school forward. Middle line supervisors working in synchrony are equivalent to an engine's cylinders working synergistically. When the school organization is running effectively for staff and students, it is important for good practices to be retained and maintained even if the principal leaves the position. Middle line supervisors knowing the laws of leadership and executing them can ensure this.

The principal, during his/her tenure, must model and explain principles that supervisors must abide by to sustain academic effectiveness. John C. Maxwell in his bestseller, *The 21 Irrefutable Laws of Leadership*, describes these principles as laws. I have adopted these laws and contend that the school principal can use them to ensure that middle line supervisors know how to carry on if the principal leaves.

I believe the following laws would be beneficial to all principals. I also believe principals must in turn be required to teach and model these laws for middle line supervisors. Doing such would essentially help to ensure that urban systems sustain stability in the event the principal leaves. John Maxwell's 21 Irrefutable Laws of Leadership are as follows:

❑ **The Law of Influence**: The supervisor should earn the respect of his teachers and encourage them to change in the direction of the school's vision, and they will do so, happily and willingly.

❑ **The Law of the Lid**: The supervisor should have the ability to lead. The lower the supervisor's ability to lead, the lower the lid. The higher the leadership skill, the higher the lid, and the greater her effectiveness is with teachers.

❑ **The Law of Process**: The supervisor invests in teachers' success, daily, by helping them grow their personal vision and school's mission. John Maxwell states that the leader [supervisor] should determine his progress via this aphorism "I grow and know; It starts to show." The supervisor's process of development is passed on to teachers.

❑ **The Law of Navigation**: The supervisor should clarify for teachers exactly what the benchmarks are for progress. The details for each benchmark should be specified. Also, the supervisor should have a listening posture in order to receive vital information that will contribute to success.

❑ **The Law of E.F. Hutton**: The supervisor should observe to see who the untitled leader is in his department. To whom do department members listen and confide. Supervisors must know these people and effectively use their talent to connect their colleagues for a specific purpose.

❏ **The Law of Solid Ground**: The supervisor should maintain the trust of his teachers. He should consistently engage them in the decision-making process. More importantly, he must reveal early on how decisions will be made. The supervisor's consistency in the decision-making process earns him trust, which is essential in the leadership process.

❏ **The Law of Respect**: The supervisor should be perceived by teachers as one who is strong. Respect is given to supervisors who demonstrate will and effective skill to attain established goals.

❏ **The Law of Intuition**: The supervisor should be able to delve into his leadership process, and arrive at valid conclusions by having a keen sense of situations, interpreting accurately, teachers' and staff responses and addressing them accordingly.

❏ **The Law of Magnetism**: The supervisor must have clarity of qualities he possesses. It is also important for him to have positive qualities because he will attract people unlike himself. Supervisors who attract teachers of similar ilk have those people on his side to get the work done.

❏ **The Law of Connection**: It is in the supervisor's best interest to know the qualities that help them connect with teachers. Teachers respond when the supervisor shows passion and compassion in the leadership process. Demonstrating insight and confidence earns the leader support from his teachers as well. The use of humor, as it naturally fits the supervisor's character, can add a dimension in making connections with teachers. A basic rule for supervisors should be to manage affairs with their heads, but lead with their heart.

❑ **The Law of the Inner Circle:** Supervisors should develop competent and qualified teachers in their inner circle. The effectiveness of teachers who make up any inner circle depends on the degree that each individual develops his or her leadership qualities.

❑ **The Law of Empowerment:** In order for supervisors to have power, they must give it away.

❑ **The Law of Reproduction:** The goodness that emerges from the supervisor is replicated through those with whom she works, that is, if the practices of the supervisor evolve from solid skills.

❑ **The Law of Buy-In:** When teachers connect with the supervisor because they believe in her, then they will support the vision.

❑ **The Law of Victory:** Supervisors must know that "winning" and success" are relative. Teachers should be informed that little victories are victories just the same.

❑ **The Law of Big Mo:** "Momentum is a Leader's Best Friend." Someone once said that too much analysis leads to paralysis. Supervisors should inform teachers that motivation and positive actions are essential habits in the educational process. This action allows for progress even in the midst of obstacles.

❑ **The Law of Priorities:** Aimless energy has no specific purpose. Supervisors should ensure that first things are done first as Stephen Covey would say. The supervisor should spend his time communicating, leading, creating, and networking with teachers.

❑ **The Law of Sacrifice:** Supervisors should have insight that moves them to make decisions that do not align with normal procedures considered by teachers, particularly when he believes the decisions will be in the best interest of the program.

❑ **The Law of Timing:** John Maxwell states that supervisors not only need to know when to lead, but they must know what to do and where to go. Thinking on his or her feet is a must.

❑ **The Law of Explosive Growth:** The faster supervisors can develop teachers, better will the chance be for the department to be effective.

❑ **The Law of Legacy:** Old folk would say "Let the work I've done speak for me." Supervisors who have been successful supporting and developing teachers will not have to speak of their deeds, for their deeds will speak for them via teachers and staff who have benefited.

Finally, principals who ensure that middle line supervisors master these laws and demonstrate them in the supervisory process will increase the possibility of the school's capacity to be successful. The school's success is contingent on those who are committed over time. These people are the Dreyans, the finishers. Middle Line Supervisors who effectuate essential practices with teachers increase the path toward school success even if the principal leaves the position.

As I flew back to Baltimore from my trip to Bathe, Maine I felt that the experience was both informing and confirming. I realized from my conversations and observations that establishing and sustaining a vision for a school had to be strategically done. The process was now in my mind.

* * * * * * * * *

Watch your thoughts, because your thoughts become your actions; watch your actions because your actions become your habits; watch your habits because your habits become your character; watch your character because your character will become your destiny.
Author Unknown

CHAPTER THREE

PORTABLE CONCEPTS

- The vision of the school must be clear and accommodate stakeholders of the school; then the stakeholders will be energized to participate in the mission of activities aligned to accomplish the vision.

- The principal must know his customers and what they want so that he can keep their expectations in mind while leading the school stakeholders toward the vision.

- The principal must know the political environment and public policies affecting her school so that she can know what decisions she must make in keeping with the vision.

- The principal must build capacity in his school by training middle line supervisors to motivate and influence teachers toward practices that produce academic excellence for students.

INTERPERSONAL RELATIONSHIPS

The first step in the acquisition of wisdom is silence, the second listening,
the third memory, the fourth practice, the fifth teaching others.
Solomon-Ibn Gabriel

WHY MUST STAFF AND STUDENTS PERCEIVE THE PRINCIPAL AS AN HONEST PERSON?

The "power" administrators have to encourage others is related to specific attributes: honesty, competence, and inspiration as noted by authors James Kouzes and Barry Posner in their book, *Credibility.*

Colleagues often ask me how I am able to command the attention of so many students at once—2,100 students during any one mass assembly to be exact. In response, I tell my colleagues that I develop appropriate relationships with my students in 100 groups of 21; so that when they are in larger groups they realize that the same person is calling for their attention.

I was actually exposed to skills that help develop interpersonal relationships while in my counselor education program at Penn State University. Skills such as listening, (i.e. paraphrasing, reflecting, feeling) truth telling, and connecting helped me greatly as I moved into the field of administration. I have been told, often, by my staff that they appreciate my honesty. I must readily admit that the honesty that resides deep inside of me emanates because of the skills I have acquired in the counseling field.

Administrators who effectively connect with staff and students using power relative to the attributes sited above will help move their schools toward a state of excellence. However, administrators and staff members *must readily assume the responsibility of guiding* students toward the mark of excellence. Honesty is one attribute that helps all participants move toward excellence. As this chapter progresses I will explain why.

I have learned that honesty is not optional. Rather, it is a quality the Principal must possess. It is the foundation upon which positive relationships are established. Administrators who are honest gain the confidence of others. Staff and students easily confide in people they perceive as honest. They also are more likely to seek guidance from them. Administrators who are fundamentally honest can have this attribute benefit them greatly by acquiring the skills that will help them communicate this most significant quality.

Staff members also appreciate when administrators make an honest attempt to understand the job from a staff member's perspective. Employees, like others, feel that you don't understand their reality unless you have "walked a mile in their shoes." Students more readily trust adults who honestly attempt to understand the world from the students' perspective.

In 1974, anthropologist John Ogbu stated that one should not confirm that he understands a specific group or culture of people unless the understanding is from their perspective. Sociologists explain this same concept another way. They use the term "social distance." Social distance connotes how far sociologists are from understanding the realities of those being studied. The more accurate sociologists are in explaining behaviors, attributes and values of a group, the shorter the distance is between what is perceived and what is real.

Urban administrators and their staff members must understand this same social distance concept when working with students. For example, many students in urban America perceive discipline without relationship in general to be offensive. In other words, a particular student might detest a command from an adult such as, "you will bring a notebook to school," even though, it is clearly evident that this directive is in the best interest of the student. Adults who work with young people should not misread students' response to this caring request to be their disdain for education, but rather their possible misunderstanding about the significance of such a request. The question here is: Why do students not respond to adult guidance which for the most part is in their best interest?

I will not take the time here to go into a psychological, sociological, or cultural explanation. However, I will present the method to effectively address students who are offended when adults merely make reasonable requests or suggest good advice. Dr. Jacqueline Brown stated in a workshop held in Maryland's Prince George's County Public School System that students' belief is, "Anybody who can't treat me right can't teach me right."

I have observed that when adults do not develop a relationship with students, students perceive discipline as something being done *to them* as opposed to *for them*. One might ask: "Why should administrators and teachers have to develop a relationship with students? They might further state, "Students should come to school ready to learn." I would say that there is a sense of readiness and focus students should have when they arrive to school. However, for various personal reasons, whether we understand them or not, many do not come with a focused mindset. Subsequently, relationship building is a skill that must be a part of teachers' and administrators' repertoires.

Another important point to note is students seem more receptive to messages from the people who reside in their communities. Today, faculty and staff often do not live in the students' community. I have frequently experienced students responding to messages I gave them only after an adult from the community sanctioned my authority and credibility. The implication of this phenomenon is that individuals who are perceived as being a part of the community can influence the attitude and behavior of students. It is therefore encouraged that school officials, to the extent they can, make an effort to become a part of the community from which their students come.

In order to develop a healthy, working relationship with students, adults must demonstrate their concern for students. Adults must get into what William Glasser calls their *Quality World* and reciprocally put students into their own. An individual's quality world contains pictures or perceptions of people, things, and situations that are of high quality about which he/she has learned to feel especially good.

Building rapport with students is also essential. Tony Robbins, author of several books about interpersonal relationships, states that the key to building rapport is flexibility. Teachers willing to experience the world as students do gain students' confidence.

Principals and administrators often face situations where parents articulate concerns about their children, teachers have concerns about students, student express their thoughts and feelings about teachers and parents; and superintendents express their displeasure about events and/or communications related to "occurrences" in the schoolhouse. Principals have to invoke flexibility as an extension of rapport to concerns of those with whom they interact from their perspective.

Given the inevitability of concerns expressed by teachers, students, parents, and superintendents, I encourage administrators to subscribe to a process that allows them to decrease stress, and to invoke confidence that these consistent and unavoidable concerns can be dealt with competently. I propose a standard procedure in which the Principal learns to understand several variables: (1) the role of the stakeholder (2) the Principal's ability to bring parity to situations, (3) and finally his skill to gather information in order to make informed decisions.

Principals must <u>know</u> their customers (parents, students, business leaders, and bosses) well. To know these groups is to understand their psychology. I would like to pause here to define more poignantly the notion of knowing the customer. The benefit of having my mother for thirteen years helps with the definition. On several occasions growing up in Baltimore, I would bring my "friends" to my house. They would be allowed to move freely; for the manners and hospitality we were taught by my mother made them welcomed to do so. It was only after my "friends" left that my mother would have a heartfelt talk with me.

My mother would say, "Don't bring that boy back to this house. That child is bad news." In other words, my mother's life experience combined with her ability to observe well, her instincts which some people call the spirit of discernment, and her decision to error on the side of caution, moved her to say, "… that child is bad news."

In most instances where my mother injected her knowledge about my friends, time proved she was right. I believe, therefore, that principals must know their parents, students and others the way my mother knew – via "mother wit" – which calls for good observation combined with life experiences, instinct, and decisiveness. When principals understand the thought process of their customers they can serve them more effectively.

Principals are managers of both <u>fact</u> and <u>fiction</u>. It is crucial, therefore, for principals to distinguish between incidents that depict factual and fictitious constructs and manage both. Distinction between these two concepts allows the principal to be fair in his decisions. Finally and closely aligned with the previous thought is the principal's confidence to make decisions after distinguishing clearly factual and fictitious information.

The principal can position herself to be understood by all concerned. Adults who have proactively placed themselves in a child's life have inevitably positioned themselves to have a positive influence on the child's educational experience. Consequently, the young person maintains a favorable impression of the adult —one that will have a long-lasting and constructive effect on the sustained quality of life for the child.

Adults who find themselves within a student's quality world are usually those who listen to students and allow them to positively express themselves. Students believe some of what we say and more of what we do as adults. Remember! As Lisa Delpit stated in her book, we are teaching *Other People's Children.*

The Benefits of Perceived Honesty

While serving as Principal at Greenspring Middle School, we emphasized to students that telling the truth was paramount. Students were informed that the truth is their primary guide and that there are benefits in telling the truth. For example, we would say that the truth can make you free.

I recall an incident where students were misbehaving in a classroom where a substitute teacher was in place. When I entered the classroom, students began telling me that someone in the back of the room was shooting paper with a rubber band. I proceeded to ask about the culprit. Obviously, no one knew initially. I gave the back section of the class detention, informing the culprit that he/she still had time to come forward. The student later came forward. She said that she was initially afraid to do so, but she honored the mutual respect between us and the mutual respect was what prompted her to come forward.

Here again, we see how relationship building is essential. Once the entire faculty works to establish relationships with students, the rules used to punish students will be needed less.

Often, the children we teach come from home situations where their attitudes and social development vary from positive to negative experiences. Thus, our only opportunity to develop a relationship is through our verbal exchanges and modeling. These interactions and modeled behaviors are more believable when they are seen as honest and consistent.

Learning students' names is another avenue to building relationships with them. In so doing, sound relationships are established between staff and students, along with the opportunity to build trust and be perceived as honest and fair.

Because I essentially have 2,100 students I am attempting to get to know, I develop strategies for getting to know them. One of the key strategies I use to learn students' names is calling the person's name as many times as possible during our conversation. Why? Because it demonstrates that a connection is taking place as we converse.

I often listen in on students' conversations in the hallway or cafeteria. I especially listen for names while passing by a group of students and speaking to the student whose name I learned. Sometimes students respond, "How do you know my name?" And although they appear shocked, what I have come to believe is students really want you to know their names. One day I had a conversation with my godmother who told me that she met a student who went to my school. My godmother shared that the student showed a great deal of joy because I knew her name.

As administrators, we usually learn names of students who misbehave. We learn students' names by the number of teachers who consistently talk about a particular student's personal challenges. Or we learn students' names by the amount of times the names appear on the absentee list. We must change this by not allowing trouble to be that which acquaints us with our students. As a matter of fact, you decrease the chance of students misbehaving if they know that you know who they are–and not simply by sight recognition but by name. There is power in the name.

If, for some reason, you happen to forget a student's name simply ask him or her again and again. Again, students want you to know them by name. It shows your humanity and your interest. Showing students you are human and real can also be done by shaking a student's hand, hugging them, sitting with them at lunchtime, etc. *A word of caution is needed here.* This has become a very litigious society so make sure you use prudence when centering with students by touching, hugging, etc.

Honesty must always be evident in the administrator's interactions with staff and students. Honesty on the part of the administrator entails interacting with staff and students judiciously and truthfully relative to issues that arise within the school organization. While relating to staff and students, administrators are forced to make decisions. Decisions call for the principal to choose among competing issues. As a result of choosing, staff and student aspirations or expectations are sometimes given second priority or are dismissed totally. Even when democratic means for making decisions are used, those whose ideas are not favored, feel disappointed.

Another major factor regarding the administrator being perceived as honest is the consistency with which decisions are made, particularly about similar issues and situations. Inconsistency by administrators provides a window of opportunity for staff and students to debate decision making. Administrators sometimes need to change from a position that was formerly established in a decision-making process. This must be done openly so that those involved in the earlier decision can maintain their confidence and continue to perceive the administrator as honest.

Perceived honesty of the administrator is essential when leading in a school. Many obstacles arise when honesty does not exist. Oba T' Shaka, expands the idea of the leader (principal) connecting with those he leads to a community/society construct, and captures the essence of the leader centering with those whom he interacts. In *The Art of Leadership* he states, "Go to the people; live with them; learn from them; love them; plan with them. Start with what they know. Build on what they have."

> **HOW DOES THE PRINCIPAL'S COMPETENCY CONTRIBUTE TO ESTABLISHING INTERPERSONAL CONNECTION WITH STAFF?**

Competent administrators employ every opportunity to make strides toward school excellence. Staff members who believe in the principal will follow and contribute to enacting the vision. Principals must show administrative acumen when it comes to having an insight about all of the dimensions of the school program. Administrators should also be able to coach staff members regarding school climate, curriculum, parent, and personal management issues. Leaders who coach staff members or provide instances for them to be coached regarding school initiatives, build a foundation upon which an accountability measure can be established.

Staff members more readily accept accountability after they have been shown what and how to do a particular task. Administrators must also demonstrate tolerance as staff members acquire skills and execute behaviors that are in accordance with the school's goals. Those in the school organization who are ineffective must be monitored closely and counseled accordingly.

Wyatt Coger, a former supervisor, shared with me and other administrators that staff members should believe in you to the degree that you can get them to "walk on water" if asked to do so. In essence, what Mr. Coger was saying is the leader's competence in connecting with staff members and valuing them should motivate staff to attempt those things that are extraordinary.

Many administrators unfortunately avoid connecting with staff and students because they have bought into the vertically linear superordinate leadership paradigm. In other words, the principal sits atop everyone and cannot move beyond a stoic and perfunctory relationship with his staff and students. On the contrary, administrators who connect with staff members beyond the mechanical supervisor/supervisee relationship, within ethical boundaries, however, seemingly inspire their staff to do those things which otherwise are perceived to be extraordinary.

HOW DO WE INSPIRE STUDENTS AND TEACHERS TO ACT POSITIVELY TOWARD ACHIEVING SCHOOL GOALS?

As administrators, we often say, *"I'm tired of saying the same thing to this employee or student—particularly when it relates to them following protocol and procedures within certain parameters in the school."*

I think it is normal for anyone giving guidance or direction to feel those receiving it should readily follow through. As a matter of fact, I like you, have experienced that follow-through behavior does not always happen. At the same time, I have learned that there are many reasons for this. The reasons for lack of follow through can range from lack of comprehension to obstinacy.

For example, I have experienced on many occasions professionals (teachers, administrators, etc.) not admitting that they misunderstood a request or not able to execute a request because they lack knowledge and skill. Simply speaking, they were too proud to ask. On the other hand, there are those who refuse to honor requests made by administrators because they are personally stubborn.

Action research has taught me that administrators and school leaders have to be "preachers," "teachers," and "technicians" in order to make certain that staff, students, and other stakeholders receive and adopt policies that are designed to achieve school goals.

The principal as "preacher" consistently addresses issues and realities directly related to the inspiration of students and staff to act positively, and to achieve tasks for which they are held responsible. In schools where I have served as an administrator, I used grade level or team meetings to engage students and inspire them toward school goals or address certain issues relevant to school. These same meetings are called, *Student Convert Meetings*, in a later chapter. Some of the issues discussed are directly related to behavior and/or student attitudes.

Principals can also use this preaching concept when focusing on strategies and activities in the School Improvement Plan. As referenced in an earlier chapter, anything introduced to an individual's mind over and over becomes real. Thus, the principal's preaching about school policies also becomes real. A key component in preaching is the perceived validity and clarity by those listening.

For example, staff and students must perceive the message in the "sermon" as truthful about implementing a specific strategy. Here is a case and point. The principal must consistently state to teachers that in order for us to positively affect students' academic and social/emotional growth, we must know them by their name and need. When staff members buy this as truth, then those activities necessary to learn students' particular needs become perceived as part of what they must do to help students.

The principal as "teacher" realizes in the teaching and learning situation that the learner is more motivated to participate when the teacher (leader) speaks to his reality or needs. When the principal helps the student understand something about self, the student's willingness to try is increased.

Another example, let's take a special needs student with a specific learning disability who is in a math class. The teacher increases the chance of keeping this student motivated if she builds a rapport with the student, helps him understand his progress, and uses concepts during the teaching process which are relevant to the students' life experiences.

A former headmaster once said to me, "Real teachers do not teach subjects, they teach students." From their mastery or lack of mastery of the content, students are able to assess where they are. A principal's role is to help students through the educational process of self-assessment. Students' efforts to succeed are increased when they are convinced that they are not allowed to fail because of the caring adults and their nurturing school environment.

Finally, the principal as "technician" must understand and act relative to the socio-cultural and socio-political issues that affect their students. Dr. Jeff Howard, chairperson and CEO of the Efficacy Institute, has gathered sound research theories that can be used by individuals or groups who must bring a positive and moral action to bear in order to contend with circumstances in society that are often oppressive.

Dr. Howard starts with the definition of efficacy, and his definition states that:

"Efficacy involves individuals executing behaviors where they are morally able to solve problems and promote development. School administrators should be able to convey to their students concepts that make them take responsibility and ownership for changing any negative or undesirable circumstances in their environment. Activities promoted by the school should attempt to connect the school to the community, until such time that community members are mobilized to support students in the community in preparation for school."

I believe that the school is a community. Dr. Robert Schiller, an Interim CEO of Baltimore City Public Schools, often stated the following sociological concept: "The school can only rise as high as the community." An example of bringing the school and community together can be explained in this idea. As a principal/technician, I have envisioned churches in the community opening up their doors and reaching out to help families with their particular problems. Within this effort by churches, I am not exclusively suggesting that churches enlist and convert families in the community to the faith. I do, however, see churches assisting directly or indirectly, individual families and members with real problems and the issues they face.

Bethel A.M.E in Church in Baltimore, for example, has a Community Outreach Center. Within this center families are assisted in a number of ways. Those with drug and alcohol addictions assist each other using life principles of the Bible and information from 12 Step Programs for narcotics and alcohol abuse. This outreach center also feeds the homeless and provides clothes and clothing vouchers. Programs provided by the Bethel Outreach Center for that local school community could serve as role models for churches in other communities.

If the vision for the school is going to be continually expanded, organizations in the community must assist families of students who attend the school. "Preaching" to students and staff, "teaching" them, and "reaching" for them as a principal/technician, serves as a collective and genuine gesture of concern. These processes also serve as a method that, when done programmatically, provides a conduit through which inspiration can occur.

Finally, although this chapter focused on inspiring teachers and students by "preaching" to them, "teaching" to them, and serving as "technicians" for them, I suggest that principals also create dialogues with students and teachers. Even if the exchange between the Principal and student or adult becomes heated, the principal should reflect on what is being said to pull the good from it, if there is any.

* * * * * * * * *

Human interpersonal connection by the leader is essential given people's psychological and emotional need to be extolled. However, decisiveness by the leader is equally necessary regardless of unpopularity of the choice.
Unknown

PORTABLE CONCEPTS

- An interpersonal connection between the principal and staff and students can serve as a powerful management tool to get things done within the school organization.

- Honesty is a perception determined by students and staff, grounded by the consistency of what the principal articulates and demonstrates.

- Students usually will demonstrate appropriate behavior for adults who establish a relationship with them by listening and being flexible.

- Staff and students have interests that make them susceptible to being inspired. The principal must connect and center with the realities of staff and students and methodically encourage them toward their interests.

CHAPTER FIVE

STUDENT DISCIPLINE

Discipline should not be practiced like a rule imposed on oneself from the
outside, but that it becomes an expression of one's own will; that it is felt as
pleasant, and that one slowly accustoms oneself to a kind of behavior that one
would eventually miss, if one stopped practicing it.

Erich Fromm

WHAT STRATEGIES CAN BE USED TO EFFECTIVELY DISCIPLINE STUDENTS IN SCHOOL?

Often, I engage in philosophical conversation about urban education with Kevin Brisbon and Roger Shaw; two of my closest friends and astute colleagues. Kevin is a coordinator of a special education program, and Roger is a principal of a high school; both are employed by the Baltimore City Public School System.

In this chapter, I have attempted to recapture conversations that Kevin and I have had relative to different topics. While our discussions will not be chronicled verbatim, the precision in revisiting Kevin's ideas relative to mine will be pretty accurate. For it was always the case that

Kevin would pose the question something like, "Drey, what do you think about...?"

HELL NO . . .

One fall school day near the close of the quarter for student grade reporting, a high school principal announced to the student body that they would return to their homeroom classes to receive their report card. When the students were asked to return, they vehemently defied the request. In concert, as a matter of fact, they chanted, "Hell no, we won't go," repeatedly. The principal asked them several times to return to their homeroom, but the students persisted in their defiance. The decision was made by the principal to place all students— approximately 1,000—on suspension to restore order and discipline. It was clear to me that discipline and control was needed in the situation. The question for leaders, therefore, is the question that opens this chapter.

Although I enjoyed the benefit of listening to Kevin's wisdom on many subjects, I usually did not get the chance to do so until after I attempted to substantively respond to his question, because he seemingly probed each of my responses to no end.

Our conversation about the massive defiance experienced by my colleague highlighted in this vignette is one of the conversations that Kevin and I had. The question went something like this, "Drey, what do you think happened at...High School?" The ideas written below contain the gist of my response to Kevin.

In many urban schools across the country student discipline is an issue that all administrators, teachers and others face. It's often asked, "Why do so many students misbehave in school?" A common response to this question is, "There is no home training."

While the question seems straightforward and simplistic, the answer really begs another question in search for another answer. In short, the answer to the question is intricate, and requires a close examination by the collective of those of us who care.

Administrators, from my experience, must reconstruct the duties and responsibilities of the principal in order to have a qualified voice with those who will address the spiritual, cultural, political and economic issues that answers the question, "Why do students misbehave in school?"

I will say that my action research in concert with trial and error as a principal have shown me that there are creative means for addressing student discipline in elementary, middle, and high schools in order to assist students in acquiring responsible behavior. I contend that if student discipline is effectively and collectively addressed district wide in elementary and middle schools, you can ensure that students will be better disciplined at the high school level. This does not, however, in any way, negate the need for a massive community movement to address the oppressive circumstances students face daily that contribute to their school behavior.

Furthermore, my observations have shown that students who misbehave in school either come from a family background of abuse or neglect—whether malignant or benign. When I speak of abuse here, I speak of and image students being harshly "disciplined" where both emotional and physical scars follow. Obviously, there is an absence of love and nurturing. Additionally, I also think of the horrendous acts on the part of adults, which deprive students of basic necessities.

For example, a parent who buys drugs with money that should be set aside for a child's meal is considered malignant neglect. Benign neglect, on the other hand, entails adults doing harm to children out of their ignorance or lack of information or education. Another example, a parent not giving a child proper guidance because he has not received it is considered benign neglect. Thus, when I reference education, I'm thinking about "old time" education.

This type of education entailed leadership based on community consciousness that honored the status of the elder. Out of this culture evolved parents who expected students to excel merely because education was important. As I reflect upon my own life, my mother was a woman who had only a fifth grade education, yet I can still hear her saying, "Boy, you better behave and go to school and get your education."

While this culture of education is slowly changing in urban communities, particularly in Black communities, administrators must establish strategies that will help discipline students in school. Student discipline strategies should be created with the input of parents, teachers and essential stakeholders.

The ideas I present here were in response to Kevin's questions, and while the constant probing and follow-up questions are not written here believe me when I tell you that they did exist during our original dialogue.

PRINCIPLE CENTERED SCHOOLS

Beating Kevin to the punch this time, he did not get a chance to ask me a question. I was so excited about the new information I read about principle-centered schools, I eagerly talked about its application. I started out discussing the symptoms of oppression (i.e. poverty, crime, neglect, etc) that usually affect the school age child's behavior. I shared my belief that it is essential for urban schools to be principle-centered. To strengthen my position, I offered that Stephen Covey would say, "A principle-centered school is a place where adults and students work toward self-discipline and self-mastery as a life goal." I believe the attitudes and behaviors demonstrated by individuals who learn to master themselves could be summed up with one word: *character.*

If students are to acquire character, guiding principles must be introduced to them and consistently reinforced by the adults working with them. It is also important that teachers guide their own behavior, referencing principles and character building concepts in the process. I emphasized to Kevin that this was crucial. With character building principles as the core, the opportunity for goal attainment is greatly increased.

The fundamental premise of student discipline is that there is a consequence for every behavior. In other words, an adult's action should be in consonance with the act demonstrated by the student. When students exhibit positive behavior they should be praised and acknowledged accordingly. However, if students' behavior is such that it falls outside the student code of conduct, the adult's action should appropriately address students' behavior.

The goal for adults in the school environment is to set students up to succeed. Ensuring students' success is done by creating an environment where students believe they are cared for and will not be allowed to fail. Once this basic premise is established in the school, other programs, policies or activities can be created to ensure student discipline throughout the school. I have observed it is sometimes difficult to get all adults to enforce student discipline policies and procedures. Yet all adults must be on board to discipline students. This is indeed a chore for the principal.

Character Education Counseling Assistance (CECA)

Kevin and I reflected on the programs, policies, and activities established at Greenspring Middle School where we both worked. I also alluded to similar school management activities used at Walbrook High School Uniform Services Academy that helped to solidify student discipline.

While serving as principal of Greenspring Middle School during the spring of 1997, staff members and I brainstormed about how to decrease office referrals. We concluded that we would designate a staff member as the Character Education Counseling Assistant (CECA) for each of the three floor administrators.

The administrators went on to discuss the specific role the CECA would have in the school-wide discipline process. The CECA was defined as an individual who helped students reflect on their behaviors so that they would act within the boundaries of the school discipline code. Essentially a CECA responsibility was to be proactive. In being proactive, this person would move in and out of classrooms supporting both teachers and students. The support for teachers would be given by addressing the students' negative attitudes and behaviors.

A critical tool for the CECA was the Progressive Discipline Process. At Greenspring Middle School, whenever a disruptive student needed to be disciplined, he or she was put through the Progressive Discipline Process, which is outlined below:

First, the student's name is placed on the chalkboard and the teacher states, "Jamal, your behavior is interfering with your education as well as your classmates' education." If the student's misbehavior persisted, the teacher applied the second step in the process. The second step was reminding the student of his behavior and having him either write a description of his behavior or move to an area of the room for timeout to reflect on the same. The third step in this process involved the student being sent to another teacher's classroom on the team with an assignment. If a student continued to misbehave in the other teachers' classroom the fourth step was applied. The fourth step was an administrative referral. Once the student was referred to the administrator, she determined whether to place the student on disciplinary removal or send him to the CECA. The goal of the CECA is to help the student identify, clarify, and rectify behavior.

As an additional note regarding the Progressive Discipline Process, a student is only afforded an opportunity to be involved in it if his behavior falls into what is called, the *Persistent Disobedient* category of the school code. Persistent Disobedience is considered behavior that is minor in nature. For example, disrespect, profanity, insubordination, etc. On the other hand, there are behaviors that are deemed to be *Gross Misconduct* in nature, as in the case of drug distribution, carrying weapons, fighting, etc. Student behaviors that are judged to be in this category are subject to immediate expulsion.

Kevin and I talked about progressive discipline versus zero tolerance. I explained how I thought the goal of student discipline in the early and middle grades is to train students to behave within a student code of conduct. Therefore, it is essential to give students opportunities to change inappropriate behaviors. It is also a reality in public education that if students are constantly sent home on disciplinary removal for a behavior categorized as persistent disobedience, they will merely come back to school after a few days of wanted vacation without any understanding of why that behavior is inappropriate or unproductive in the learning environment, and a revolving door is established.

A progressive discipline process, on the other hand, gives the adults in the school an opportunity to help students change their behavior, while simultaneously documenting the same in the event there is a need to eventually refer the student for another school placement.

MIRRORS

Kevin and I both concurred that the use of mirrors at Greenspring was effective. Mirrors were used to help students, first of all, own their misbehaviors. I observed students attributing their problems and conflicts to everything and everybody outside of them. Thus, an initial step before conferencing with a student about an incident might require a trip to the mirror with the following instructions: "Take responsibility for your actions and involvement in all situations. Look at the person responsible."

The mirrors were also used for reflection. Sometimes students were requested to stand in front of the mirror to think about minor misbehaviors that breached school policy. This mirror strategy taught me that students do not like to look at themselves when they feel "ugly." As effective as I found the mirror strategy to be, I believe that the strategy is age appropriate for middle and elementary school age students. While mirrors can be used in high school, the strategy, again, I believe, is most effective with middle and elementary students.

TRAFFIC LIGHT CONCEPT

While serving as principal of Walbrook High School, a committee of psychologists, teachers, and social workers expressed to me their concerns about students' impulsivity and rage when interacting with their peers and adults. During one of our meetings, a colleague suggested the traffic light concept.

We all came to the conclusion that this concept would have some usefulness in helping our students focus on self-control. In the meeting, we defined what the three colors on the traffic lights meant to us and what we needed to make them mean to our students.

Borrowing the idea that originated from the traffic light, we concluded that the red signal meant for students to merely stop; yellow indicated that the student should slow down and go through a decision-making process, e.g. think of options, think of consequences, etc., and finally green meant the student should proceed with the derived decision! After the preliminary work was done, the concept was implemented.

THE SILHOUETTE PROGRAM

Kevin had confidence in the Silhouette Program. He respectfully telephoned me and asked for "permission" to initiate a similar program where he worked. Before we hung up the phone, I was asked to generally share the basic philosophy of the program. I obliged and shared that the term silhouette was chosen because we determined that students who misbehaved possessed potential to be positive, however, their failure to use their skills and talents gradually dimmed and distorted their *being* until their true features were *gone,* and they became mere Silhouettes.

Thus to regain their features, Silhouettes were required to successfully complete a strict disciplinary process. Within this process, students' conduct, class work, and homework were monitored. Students were given the option of receiving excellent or unsatisfactory. By the way, their teachers could recommend students to the program after opportunities to monitor and correct their behavior failed.

Professionals met with students every morning during the homeroom period. Students were encouraged to exhibit positive behavior throughout the day. Although we did not have the personnel to service our students, it was recommended that Silhouettes receive an advocate to monitor their behavior during the course of the day. The advocate could also assist students with academic issues as well. If students in the Silhouette Program received an unsatisfactory marking by a teacher during the day, this was noted during homeroom, and disciplinary action taken.

We have noticed that this program works because students understand their behavior will be monitored daily. Students also realized that factual evidence is gathered that can be used to make administrative decisions within the scope of the school discipline code. Staff stated that the overall behavior of the students improved while in the Silhouette Program.

As stated earlier, the program has stringent requirements for students. The strictness of the program gives an opportunity to see students for who they really are—behaviorally. In other words, if students plan to change, they will. On the other hand, however, if students are wedded to negative behavior, it will be obvious and administrative action can be immediately taken. We found out that some students are wedded to their negative behavior to the point that they need advocates with them throughout the day to keep them on track.

The role of the advocate can also be expanded to help students outside of the school setting as well. Finally, students whose behavior changed positively were able to graduate from the Silhouette Program in front of their peers and receive their "features back."

KUDOS PROGRAM

The Silhouette Program is an effort by the staff and administrators to change students' misbehavior. The Kudos Program, on the other hand, acknowledges students for positive behavior. Kevin shared his admiration for this program. He noticed the excitement shown by students when they were recognized for exhibiting noteworthy behavior. Accentuating the positive was the gist of the Kudos Program.

The Kudos Program was essentially a pacesetter for positive involvement in our school. Students want to be recognized for doing good deeds. Staff members, therefore, must continue to recognize behavior that we want students to constantly actualize.

At Greenspring Middle, students received kudos for turning in lost items, doing an exceptional school project, and showing student leadership, i.e. mediating a fight, volunteering time, etc. The recognition of students usually happened via the public announcement system or in assemblies. I'd often tell students, "If you want to show off or to be seen, here is your opportunity." In other words, do something that deserves kudos.

SCHOOL UNIFORMS

Sitting in my office with Kevin one day, I shared with him how I thought school uniforms could contribute to the strategies used to provide discipline and structure within the school. I must say, merely wearing uniforms only makes a small contribution to the student discipline process. Coupled with other monitoring strategies, however, I believe school uniforms can contribute to positive student discipline in school.

For example, when all students are wearing uniforms the adults are able to identify whether or not children in the building actually attend the school.

Having students wear uniforms also gives the principal and others the opportunity to discuss uniformity. The idea of uniformity can induce *collective pride*. The pride students feel is a basis upon which the notion of unity can be promulgated. When students are identified as belonging, and they have a sense of pride, the adults in the school have a better chance of disciplining them because they are more apt to accept guidance.

THREE–WEEK INCENTIVES:
Supporting Activities & Policies for Student Discipline

I have noticed for sometime how advertisers on television exaggerate the image of things and personalities to capture the attention of the viewer. These commercial advertisements are subliminal techniques to hook viewers' minds so that they become bent on a particular product.

There are many people who wear Air Jordan shoes not because they necessarily fit comfortably, but because Michael Jordan has become synonymous with the shoe. The "thought of Michael" has a physiological effect on some people. He actually changes their mood to the point that they say, "Wow! Michael Jordan..." Well, if shoes can become associated with a created icon, honor roll students can be created to be icons as well.

Sitting on the sideline after an intense three on three basketball game, I shared with Kevin and the other teachers present that the same concept advertisers used to create superstars could be used in the school. At the schools where I served as principal, it was our intent to make honor roll students icons by glorifying them every three weeks.

These student *glory moments* took place in an assembly. The attention they receive was directly tied to their "Honor Roll" achievement. Allow me to state that *all students* are included in this process. Staff members must creatively recognize all students who are demonstrating their genuine best effort.

When students' accomplishments are glorified and incentives are attached which are of particular interest to the student, you can create a positive and productive cadre of students who will contribute to the school goals. The staff must come to know by names and deeds students who are positively contributing to the school climate, and establish these students as the trendsetters in the school. These students inevitably create the flow that you want other students to follow. Thus, programs must occur to publicly recognize them. Incentives in this process must be chosen by students in order for them to be of true interest to the student.

CODE OF CARE

Students are microcosms of communities (macrocosms). Thus, community values and behavior - positive or negative - usually find their way into school. The negative attitudes and values students learn are counter-productive in school. There is a silent student code of conduct that condones and perpetuates negative behavior.

I have observed that students, overall, do not want to condone negative behaviors that make the school environment unsafe. They also do not want to jeopardize their own safety by publicly informing the administrators about peers who breach school conduct codes. This fear is no different from the fear that grips many citizens in inner city communities across the nation. These citizens are afraid to testify and unify against criminals for fear of reprisal.

We attempted to address this code of silence issue in my middle school by instituting our own "Code of Care Policy." The term Code of Care replaces the negative idea of "snitching," "squealing," or "telling." Many students in the school deem these terms as taboo. Even when some students' behaviors are a breach of the school code and sometimes the law, others believe that it is not their obligation to "snitch." Again, this is a position taken most often out of fear.

Student anonymity is critical if the principal and his administrators expect to obtain information. As a rule, the principal must maintain student and staff safety at all costs. Therefore, I give the entire student body my pager number. I share with them that it should be used in case of emergency only, and they comply with the policy. Students also have the benefit of simply writing a note about unacceptable behaviors in or around the school without identifying themselves.

In summary, it is obvious that students want to be safe, and because of this it is important for the administration to assist in this effort by getting students involved in creating a safe school environment in a systemic way.

TOUGH LOVE

Tough love is a policy that should be personally demonstrated by administrators and staff members. Tough love can actually be considered a practice because it involves consistent interaction between adults and students.

Dr. William Glasser in his book, *Quality School*, would say, "In cases where students come from homes where there is lack of consistent discipline balanced with love, teachers and administrators must introduce students to these two elements which are essential for their becoming responsible adults."

The process of tough love can be very painful for the caring adult and the undisciplined student. For example, stringent requirements for the student at the age of eleven can be difficult if he has not experienced personal structure that challenges his being. Adults working with students, however, must persist and not become permissive to counter-productive ideas and behavior.

Dr. Glasser presents a concept, coined "Quality World", which is equally essential to tough love. Again, he defines "Quality World" as, "pictures and perceptions of people, things and situations that individuals have in their minds about which they have learned to feel especially good." Thus, tough love is valuable to the extent students place the adult in their Quality World.

Undoubtedly, tough love requires extensive training of adults if they are going to work effectively with students. As stated earlier, there must be balance between the distribution of love and discipline. Ironically, love and discipline are perceived by students as painful (unacceptable) or pleasurable (acceptable) as noted by Anthony Robbins. Let's look at some instances in Lasheil's life.

Lasheil is a child who experiences inconsistent and inappropriate consequences related to her behavior when she is at home. As a point of reference, Laishel lives with her aunt because her biological mother died. Her father does not live with her, but noticeably, he periodically visits with Laishel—particularly when he is summoned by the aunt to discipline Lasheil.

Within our structured school environment she demonstrated a rejection of love and caring behaviors given by adults and gravitated to those consequences (punishments) administered instead. Often when her teachers praised her for demonstrating positive behavior (effort) as a conditioning process toward becoming a positive person, she seemingly could not accept it. Often Lasheil opted for negative behaviors that would bring what we believed to be unwholesome consequences. In short, behaviors that we perceived to be positive were actions Laishel believed would bring her pain. On the other hand, through her inconsistent experiences with love and affection, she learned to perceive the punishing consequences (detention, raised voices, suspension) as pleasurable. Our goal then became to reverse this process through a consistent discipline and caring measure at the school.

Our observations as educators allowed us to conclude that some students actually like consequences that others might consider painful. Accordingly, during the discipline process in school, adults must be consistent so that students who have been disciplined and conditioned by inconsistent measures can experience some consistency and eventually fall into the discipline structure and meet success.

To help with this process, there are certain policies we implemented to ensure that the entire student body acknowledged our authority and accepted the consequences that were accorded to the policies.

We required our students to line-up outside in the mornings. This policy was implemented in order to ready our students for the structure of the school day. We also required students to move to all assemblies silently. I am a firm believer that if you can get students to demonstrate obedience when they are in massive groups, you can ensure obedience overall when they are in different pockets of the school.

In summary, an essential element in the tough love process is this: students must respect those serving as leaders. Kevin seemed to have had an epiphany one day. He walked into my office and confirmed Robert Glasser's theory when he stated: "Students respect those who listen to them, set limits, and are reasonably flexible." I responded, jokingly, "For real!!"

COACHING CHARACTER

A coach is defined as one who trains an athlete or team. The training concept relative to a coach has some usefulness for adults in the schoolhouse when it comes to coaching character. When one trains another, she/he consistently provides instruction and practice with a particular idea or specific task. This is what makes coaching character a doable and necessary practice in schools.

Principles related to citizenship and justice should be touted as paramount and significant within the school. Once adults and students acknowledge these principles, efforts are made by both groups to live up to them.

I have observed and spent a great deal of time coaching students during the school day as they engage in educational tasks. Like the athletic coach, teachers must revisit certain behaviors and attitudes in order to correct them when necessary. Students must be encouraged to practice certain attitudes and behaviors in a methodical way. If a student makes a statement that is deemed inappropriate, adults must hold them accountable for their behavior. If an apology is needed, teachers can help students formulate their thoughts for the apology. In essence, adults in school must be willing to consistently coach students on location. As former athletic coaches, both Kevin and I knew that this strategy worked for students.

SCHOOL CLIMATE CONTROLLERS

Research on effective schools identifies a safe and orderly school climate as essential in the school improvement process. There are several practices conducive to the school improvement process that I have deemed essential when it comes to establishing a conducive school climate. I labeled these practices, "School Climate Controllers."

The first of these I would like to mention is the **Hall Pass System.** Some faculty and staff members take for granted the need for a system that accounts for the number of students in the hall at any given time. Teachers and staff members are primary insurers of the effectiveness of the Hall Pass System. Those who distribute hall passes must be mindful to whom they are distributed and the time frame in which it is done. Students who receive passes must use the privilege responsibly. A part of this responsible behavior entails not abusing time needed to take care of school business while using the pass.

There are essential elements that should be on the pass; the time the pass is given, the destination, the student's name, and the teacher's signature. It is important to note that teachers must determine the approximate time needed to take care of business while the pass is in use. I learned from one of my colleagues that a fifteen minute rule could be added to the pass system. This entails no hall passes being written during the first or last fifteen minutes of any period, or during the first and last forty-five minutes of any school day. Finally, another feature to control the climate is the time given to students to pass between classes. I allot three minutes and thirty seconds. This rule helps to keep students who linger in the halls focused and moving to their destination.

Another Climate Controller is **After School Detention**. William Glasser states that, "Children who experience discipline, tempered with caring and fairness, develop over time a stable disposition." The institution of detention in a school environment serves as a disciplinary consequence that students experience for breaking a rule. This consequence subsequently is used to help control the school climate. Detention can be used as an alternative to suspension for students who need structure and guidance.

I will assign a student multiple days of detention as opposed to sending him home on suspension. Keeping students in school, particularly those who do not have family support, gives the school staff an opportunity to engage students in activities and thinking processes that will help them demonstrate appropriate behaviors.

An In-School Suspension Center also contributes to controlling the school climate. Students who break rules are removed from their normal school schedule and placed in the center to do both their schoolwork and pay the consequence for breaking a school rule. **In-School Suspension** has the same purpose as multiple days of detention, i.e., keeping students engaged in the school process.

Finally, following excitable moments (e.g. fun activities or fights), I use the **Meditating Moment** to signal for school calmness. During the mediating moment, soft music is piped through the public address system. Students are requested to meditate, pray, etc., but they must refrain from talking. Restoring serenity after galvanic moments helps to control the school climate.

Controlling the school climate is essential for all other business to effectively take place. A safe and peaceful school environment, I contend, is the seed out of which grows mutual respect between students and adults. An additional benefit of discipline policies and rules is that they help to weed out and identify students who are maladjusted. If maladjusted behavior is not addressed, it will destroy the climate of the school and undermine a full focus on student academic achievement, which is the primary order of business in the schoolhouse.

Reemphasizing rules and procedures is essential in controlling the climate. Integrating praise and highlighting positive behaviors in this process are important so as to avoid zoning in on negativity. However, the primary factor in controlling the school climate is effectively initiating activities identified as climate controllers, and enforcing school rules and policies as they have been written, while understanding that good judgment should always be used when enforcing any rule.

DIAGRAM 6   School Climate Controllers

TYPE	PURPOSE
Hall Pass System	A system that accounts for the number of students in the hall at a given time.
After School Detention	A fair consequence designed to remind students of inappropriate actions as well as deter students from those actions.
In-School Suspension	A place to remove students from regular educational programming for disciplinary reasons, while giving him/her a structured academic program in school
Meditating Moment	A melodious musical moment where everyone in the school stops to address chaos. Everyone is directed to: listen, meditate, pray, be still and not talk.

STRATEGICALLY LOCATING PEOPLE

A major key to ensuring a safe and orderly environment is to make sure that policies and procedures envelop student behavior when they walk through the door. School policies must be clear and known by all students. Students must understand that every second of their school day is governed by policy. Adults should encourage responsible behavior so that students' participation in school is free from the consequences of breaching school policy.

Finally, I advocate strategically placing staff in specific areas of the schoolhouse to direct students and secure them if needed. I told Kevin that my support of the idea of locating people is to help gauge how much students have internalized to do what's right relative to school policies.

Adults are able to make this determination by removing people from strategic areas and monitoring the activity. If negative activity diminishes, then students are internalizing policies and procedures. On the other hand, if negative activity increases, then the converse is true; that is, students are not internalizing rules and procedures.

* * * * * * * * * *

If you can win complete mastery over self, you will easily master all else. To triumph over self is the perfect victory.
Thomas A. Kneed

PORTABLE CONCEPTS

- The principal should structure school programs in ways that remind students of their responsibilities and ultimately cause them to take it upon themselves to execute them.

- Principals must administer consistent consequences for student behaviors – good and bad – in a timely fashion.

CHAPTER FIVE

- All stakeholders must know and be clear about the policies of the school. However, if the policies and rules are not enforced then they are merely words written on paper.

CHAPTER SIX

SCHOOL IMPACT
LEADERSHIP

The reformer must attack simultaneously on all fronts;
if he does not he can not hope to achieve more than partial success."
Aldeous Huxley

There is a scripture that proclaims, "Where there is no vision, the people will perish." Paralleling this scripture, I contend, "Where there is irrelevant curriculum focus, the people (students and staff) practice their own will." Staff and faculty within a school organization who practice their own will or as common parlance would have it, "do their own thing," work to the detriment of students since students await academic guidance from adults— especially consistent guidance.

If students and staff are not to be left to their own, there has to be standardized curriculum practices to guide them. The specificity and consistent implementation of these curriculum practices, ensured by the principal, indicate *school impact leadership.* The ideas beneath the two guide questions in this chapter provide insight that promotes impact leadership inside and outside the school.

WHAT CURRICULUM PRACTICES INCREASE THE PROBABILITY FOR ACADEMIC ACHIEVEMENT IN THE SCHOOL?

One of the first practices toward securing student academic achievement entails the principal's understanding of curriculum alignment policies. In other words, the principal must know the curriculum expectations that the federal government has for the state; the expectations the state has for the school district; and the expectations the school district has for the school's staff. Generally, the principal's understanding of state and federal curriculum mandates affords him and curriculum leaders the opportunity to focus curriculum emphasis at the schoolhouse.

For example, in the state of Maryland, there are specific minimal Mathematics and English graduation requirements for high school students. My staff and I realized that too many of our students are coming to high school from middle school without basic skills; as a result we offered remedial Math and English courses in the curriculum. While this action was fundamental for my staff regarding curriculum strategy, it should not be assumed that aspiring curriculum leaders and administrators know this. Actually, I have seen missed opportunities to remedy and help students because individuals in leadership roles did not address similar situations.

There is a need for aspiring curriculum leaders and administrators to reflect and check their understanding of the scope of the curriculum process from the state board of education to the chalkboard in the classroom. When curriculum leaders understand the whole curriculum process related to their educational milieu, they can serve as *Reflective Gatekeepers* to ensure that only practices beneficial to the educational development of students enter the schooling process.

THE REFLECTIVE GATEKEEPER

Principals who serve as *Reflective Gatekeepers* in the educational process thoughtfully prioritize curriculum experiences for students. There are many circumstances that impact school achievement in the urban setting. It is imperative for instructional leaders to reflect on ways to properly address circumstances that negatively impact student academic achievement. Instructional leaders must ensure effective curriculum alignment and establish academic excellence as the ultimate goal.

Although, there are guidelines given by the state or school districts regarding the operation of School Improvement Teams, the "policies" that evolve from these teams are self-imposed and should be seriously implemented as they are collectively agreed upon. Principals risk criticism by publicly stating school goals, particularly if he falls short of stated goals and objectives in the School Improvement Plan. When goals are not stated publicly, however, the principal is accused sometimes of not providing others the opportunity to share power and engage in the school improvement process.

My experience has taught me that it does the principal well to state, openly and publicly, goals related to curriculum and other policies. The principal's public proclamation puts responsibility on him to deliver success in accordance with stated goals.

The principal's and curriculum leader's goal accomplishments in the school improvement plan are directly linked to their understanding of the school district's curriculum mandates and policies. Usually, most school districts tout general goals that give employees direction and focus. It behooves the instructional leaders to know the goals publicized by the school district so they can align the school improvement plan with the goals. Also, curriculum leaders (especially the principal), should make certain that district mandates do not detract from the curriculum process needed at the schoolhouse to address students' needs.

For example, if the data shows that many students arrive at high school with skill deficits in reading, then principals should collectively agree to have students receive some type of credit or incentive for nontraditional but needed high school courses. Prioritizing the curriculum focus should loom large in the curriculum leader's reflections about student academic achievement.

It is crucial for principals and curriculum leaders to select goals and objectives in the school improvement planning process that are relevant to students' academic needs. Equally important to selecting school improvement goals and objectives is defining the strategies and prioritizing the activities designed to reach the goals. Definitive strategies require that curriculum leaders borrow from a medical-model: diagnose the academic problem and set forth prescriptions to attack it.

Student achievement problems are often symptomatic of the pathological oppression experienced by many of our students in the urban environment. Therefore, the principal's obligation to address this societal ill is vast. Not only must he and others in the school define relevant strategies to attack the academic problems, they must also prioritize activities to guarantee the probability of incremental student achievement. In so doing, the principal increases the confidence of all participating in the educational process and convinces them that achievement is possible.

The strategy that ensures student success and increased staff confidence entails celebrating evidence of students and staff accomplishments of learning tasks within the instructional curriculum while focusing on areas still in need of development.

For example, if test data indicates student reading scores are proficient, then this should be acknowledged by appropriately and creatively informing students and staff of their success. If student and staff excellence are to occur in urban schools, then it must be systemically grown by sagacious decisions around curriculum priorities. The following are improvement strategies and activities I have defined as important in the school improvement process.

SCHOOL CLIMATE

As a Principal in an urban setting, I have come to the conclusion that the first order of business is establishment of a school climate where all things are done decently and in order. My staff and I have used activities related to metaphors and images to obtain and maintain a school climate that is safe and orderly. Metaphors are cliches, aphorisms, and slogans students and adults hear and use to direct and guide students.

Images are observable objects that adults use to focus students' attention in the educational process. In the Student Discipline and Convert Meeting chapters, I present metaphors and images used to bring about and enhance school order.

LESSONS & LIMITS

At the high school where I serve as principal we state daily to students this metaphor: "We do that Triple L Thing in here. We set <u>limits</u>, teach <u>lessons</u>, and we do it all in the name of <u>love</u>." Not only is this metaphor stated during morning announcements, it is stated during the course of the day by those who deem it appropriate.

Clear rules with known consequences are set as boundaries in which we encourage students to operate. As principal, I do not assume that students will automatically operate within established limits. I use every opportunity available to reinforce rules. I also encourage and train my staff to do the same. Refer to the chapter on Student Discipline to read some of the activities I have used to set limits for students.

I think it is important for students to master the subjects taught that are required to eventually graduate from high school. However, I have discovered the manner in which teachers get students to focus on the subject is paramount. I have read and heard somewhere that, "Good teachers teach subjects; great teachers teach children."

As stated in the previous chapter, I was blessed in the fall semester of 1994 to go to Bath, Maine where this idea was practiced at the Hyde School. The original Head Master of the school was Mr. Joe Gauld. He and the adults in the school collectively believe that the school subject helps students reach their unique potential. In his book, *Character First,* Joe Gauld writes:

> "Teachers and students use the subject as a tool to further the development of the student's unique potential. This approach motivates students at a deep level, because it transforms education into something that is meaningful to them. When academic achievement becomes a means of realizing their dreams, . . . students become serious, even passionate, about learning."

Gauld presents the two following diagrams in his book to clarify his philosophy. The first diagram depicts how the teacher and subject are at the base of the educational process, molding the student at the apex. On the other hand, the second diagram shows the teacher and the student

155

at the base of the educational process, both working on the subject at the apex as a tool to develop the student's unique potential. The process depicted in the second diagram has transforming power, especially for the student.

When students know a caring and astute human being is with them to engage the learning process, they are encouraged to persist because assistance is near if needed. The underlying reality in this process is that two animated humans can outwit an inanimate subject by working smart. On the other hand, the first diagram shows how the teacher and subject work on the student. This process can be frustrating for the student if the teacher poses the information in the subject as a challenge for the student to overcome without appropriate intervention and encouragement.

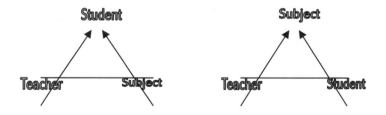

It is still my goal, even as I write this book, to educate my staff to understand the reality of the urban child and use their subjects to motivate and teach them. I believe this is a crucial practice in the process of teaching students lessons that will contribute to an orderly school climate and ultimately student academic achievement. I also believe an effective teacher uses his subject as a mirror to reflect the students' progress relative to mastering the subject and developing as a person.

A student's understanding or misunderstanding during the learning process is an indicator of the student's control or lack of control over his feelings and thinking. For example, a student who feels he's failing will be in a dilemma either to continue to try and achieve or to quit. Either decision is an indication of the degree of his personal development and control.

A teacher who is *student-centered* rather than *subject-centered*, can help guide the student through this dilemma by helping the student master the subject. Ultimately, however, she helps the student explore his feelings and thinking relative to quitting. In this case, the leader is a teacher of the student versus being the teacher of the subject. Thus, this process encompasses students learning valuable lessons via self-imposed limits.

LOVE

At a glance, one might conclude that this concept, "love," is inappropriate as an activity in the educational process. I assert, however, that demonstrative, but ethical love is an essential strategy in the educational process in urban schools. One of the things I mentioned in the chapter on Student Discipline is that it's easier to discipline students with whom you have relationships. Relationships with students are established by listening to them. Once we begin to listen to students, we get the opportunity to understand reality from their perspective.

Adults who effectively interact with students are able to do so because of the flexibility within their character. Stephen Covey has coined the term, Response-Ability. In essence, he is talking about an individual's ability to effectively respond to events in his life. I believe that adults working with students should develop the "Response-Ability" concept. Students can also benefit by developing the same skill. This brings me to another point. Students respond effectively and are most productive when adults create a school ambiance that gives students confidence that they will not be allowed to fail. In other words, students are ensured that if they persist in their efforts, they will ultimately become academically successful. Remember, school impact leadership entails the principal ensuring specific and relevant practices in the curriculum process that ensure student success.

STUDENT ACADEMIC ACHIEVEMENT

Serving as a principal in Urban America, my most difficult challenge has been to help students understand and manifest their gifts and talents. As stated in Chapter One, there are seven issues (obstacles) I believe that principals must be prepared to overcome in the leadership process if student academic excellence is to be achieved. Here, I describe the academic progress that I have facilitated in the midst of obstacles mentioned in Chapter One.

Essentially, student excellence is grown when an academic remediation program gives students the opportunity to redress skill deficiencies while curriculum pacing continues. It's important here to restate that it is essential to have great teachers who teach students how to persevere and find their unique potential. Growing excellence entails creating challenging programs (e.g. Honors, Acceleration, etc.,) by child, teacher and subject, if and where necessary. This means that curriculum leaders must handpick students who have demonstrated academic readiness to participate in rigorous courses.

Teachers who are ready to challenge these students as well as themselves should also be identified. It takes the extra effort of teachers working to challenge students with a rigorous curriculum. Finally, rigorous subjects must be handpicked in order to gradually establish an academic program designed to challenge students.

The Acceleration Program should be marketed by program leaders, stakeholders, and students. The Remediation Program must be tied to the Acceleration Program so that students can smoothly move from one program to another. High academic standards must be a part of the Accelerated Program. For example, students must get exposure to the Preliminary Scholastic Aptitude Test (PSAT) and the Scholastic Aptitude Test (SAT).

At the high school where I serve as principal, I experienced students who were on the verge of dropping out of school, but used our Saturday School program to sustain their hope to finish. We provided not only remedial courses for students, but we changed their entire attitude about school. The idea of remediation, therefore, in my mind, is to provide students hope through second chance opportunities. Our Hope Program at Walbrook High School USA was dubbed – Matriculation and Remediation.

The lack of second chance opportunities in society contributes to the unproductive behavior of many urban youth throughout the country. Finally, the academic success of students is only as substantive as the academic experience. Therefore, it is imperative that teachers get training and feedback in using their subject on how to effectively teach the urban child.

CREATING AN ACHIEVEMENT ZEIGIEST

In urban schools, educators can count on political tides and administrative oscillation to foment some fury and turbulence which influences practices inside urban schools. External politics and polices threaten to destabilize the school structure, while inside the school teachers, administrators, and students are "pro-acting" or reacting to unforeseen changes. Given this seemingly inescapable turbulence, the principal and curriculum leaders must establish tranquility through effective practice, habit, and an established value system among students and staff. This value system creates a general trend or mood. I call this the *zeitgeist* in the school, because it influences the thinking and behavior of everyone.

I must emphasize here that principals who are bent on stabilizing urban schools do so at the risk of being viewed as defiant by bosses and others.

The following word equation could be useful to principals who are leading in a school. Sustained behaviors by students and staff members as they demonstrate the four elements in the equation foster the zeitgeist in the school:

EXPECTATION + EFFORT + EXCITEMENT = ENGAGEMENT

It is usually the principal's hope that both students and staff would have high *expectations* in their respective roles. Students who have high expectations predict that adults will effectively teach them. Conversely, staff who have high expectations for students believe that students' unique potential is endless. Therefore, these staff members continue to "raise the bar" for academic standards. Students who demonstrate confidence toward reaching specific academic goals reinforce the sustained *efforts* of staff. Staff members are then encouraged to find more ways to teach students who demonstrate an interest in learning. The intrigue demonstrated by both students and staff spills over to the third element in the equation—*excitement.*

Students who persevere while attaining personal academic goals usually can't contain their excitement. This excitement manifests itself in demonstrated self-efficacy, which according to Albert Bandura, is "one's belief that he can execute behavior to bring about specific outcomes." Regarding staff excitement, it has been most rewarding to watch caring and competent teachers express joy over a student who began simply to achieve academic goals.

Finally, when both students and staff have high expectations, sustained effort, and excitement in the educational process, the result is usually *engagement* in the tasks of their respective roles. The concepts of this "quadratic word equation" motivated students and staff and ultimately contributed to the zeitgeist of the school. The creation of a school's zeitgeist is not obtained without interval training and feedback. I would be remiss and misleading if I did not say here that selecting the right leaders (teachers, supervisors, and administrators) is essential to implementing the correct practices that will eventually establish the zeitgeist in the school.

I mentioned in Chapter One that leaders – particularly aspiring principals – must be properly trained on location and be given time to reflect and dialogue in the training process. I also believe goals of academic excellence in a school have a better chance of being sustained if the principal advances the vision in the school long enough for middle line supervisors to build sustaining capacity. These specific practices are indicative of school impact leadership.

PARENTAL INVOLVEMENT

The involvement of parents in the education process is essential in all school districts. The degrees to which parents are involved vary given students' grade level, socioeconomic status, and sense of responsibility. Whatever the case may be, I have come to realize that sustained parent involvement is based on a structured process in which parents see value in participating; having at the foundation something that will benefit their child. It has been my experience that if you ask for parents' help, they will give it. The contribution that parents make to the school can help with getting daily tasks done, which indirectly helps with student academic achievement.

A more in-depth discussion about parent involvement is essential at this juncture. Often parent involvement is viewed as a collective group of parents traveling and meeting at the school with staff to get information related to their children's education. Usually the school is the giver of information during these sessions. I would like to suggest parent involvement requires more than periodic meetings at the beginning, middle, and end of the school year.

Actually, parent involvement needs to be redefined and refined to garner the necessary support for students in urban schools. To their credit, a number of parents who enrolled their child(ren) in urban schools have supported their young person as expected by themselves and appreciated by school officials as well. The energy and vision of these engaged parents are attributes that need to be modeled for parents unengaged in the educational process.

Collective energy and vision by parents can be the catalyst for community empowerment; a motivational factor that can move parents to ensure that the educational process for their children serves them well. When parents obligate themselves to support the students in school, students' engagement is better sustained. Therefore, "parent" obligation to students and their schools need to be viewed as a necessary policy for urban public schools. This notion of obligation can also be expanded to include community members as well. A call for community obligation in urban schools has to be done from an ethnic perspective. The idea of giving back to those in the community from which you have come has to be touted as essential.

Pastor P.M. Smith of Huber Memorial Church here in Baltimore often states: "There are 10,080 minutes in a week. To say that *you* do not have time to obligate yourself to young people - 75 minutes a week . . . to give to children is to have your leadership and commitment to children questioned." I personally think P.M. Smith is right, especially for African Americans.

Many in the community with African American children must realize their obligation to help students develop. The "leaders" within a particular ethnic group must be "first responders" to help the progeny in the group.

Family Learning Centers have to become essential structures that help families help students. An examination of a student's family support system will alert school leaders to the kind of support a student will need in a family learning center. The family learning center focuses therapeutically on issues that help families and ultimately the student. A culturally centered therapeutic approach is highly recommended to help African American families reconnect or compensate for the dislocations in the family that affect students.

Finally, many students who attend urban schools have shown a great deal of resilience. This strength in character must not be casually acknowledged, but understood squarely so that student resilience can serve as a foundation on which students can build themselves toward a productive future. Parents who put students in unwholesome situations that call forth student resilience must be taught how their student is strong in character and have been forced by them to be so.

It is important for parents to be informed that their students merely need to know that his/her parent is there. This type of moral support is enough for many children. In fact moral support from parents or loved ones goes far in helping students focus and engage in school.

TEACHER EFFECTIVENESS

Teacher training is the most essential component in the process of establishing teacher effectiveness and school impact leadership, providing we have hired teachers who will to teach in Urban America. Training ensures that the leadership in the school has established the direction in which they want the school to go. Effective monitoring, on the other hand, gauges teachers' commitment to implement the concepts deemed essential. Interim feedback meetings related to efforts allow the leadership to determine the next steps in the training process relative to individual teachers and/or specific training modules.

Before elaborating on the processes that ensure school impact leadership, I would like to add some fundamental ideas that are essential to ensuring student academic success. First of all, the principal must keep two basic premises in mind when trying to positively impact student academic achievement:

1. Adults participate fully in the school educational process when they are virtually "guaranteed" to succeed in their roles and duties with little or no chance of failure.

2. Students will engage in the academic process when they perceive and believe that adults will not allow them to fail.

I will not go into great detail here about how to create a mindset with both adults and students to foster the belief stated in the above premises. I will, however, say that adults must engage in support groups or teams with their peers if they are to establish the belief stated in the first premise. Students will have confidence in adults who take necessary actions to understand them and who understand their confidence level in the educational process.

ADMINISTRATORS' SEVEN MENTAL PROCESSES FOR TEACHER EFFECTIVENESS AND ENSURING SCHOOL IMPACT LEADERSHIP

First, administrators' implementation of the School Improvement Plan warrants that specific teacher training be identified and prioritized on the annual staff training calendar.

Second, a careful gauge of each teacher's area of proficiency and under-developed skill level must be identified. Afterward, develop "differential training" based on the individual needs of the teachers.

For example, teachers who are good at managing their classrooms should not be made to attend a training session on classroom management. Instead, curriculum leaders should have them focus on areas of need.

Third, it is also important to ensure that teachers have colleagues within their school staff who can serve as role models in the curriculum training process. Curriculum leaders should identify the strengths of staff members, collectively, by departments. This method allows the school to have "pockets" of success to build upon.

Fourth, curriculum leaders must build departments and fortify their areas of weakness by maintaining the efforts of teachers who support their colleagues. This method is efficient because it allows for group development. This method also helps curriculum leaders to identify those individuals who are not meeting training expectations. The curriculum leaders must step in at this point to take appropriate action.

Fifth, proactive behaviors on the behalf of the principal and curriculum leaders will direct staff, and ultimately students toward academic excellence. Helpful would it also be for school leaders to establish a primary and daily activity called "Management by Walking Around" *(MBWA).* While moving in and out of classrooms, curriculum leaders document the presence or absence of specific behaviors on forms created for that purpose. Feedback then is informally given to teachers or staff about certain behaviors that were observed.

It is important to note that positive behavior should be sought while implementing MBWA. Consistent meetings should also be held to address administrative, faculty, and instructional issues; all of which really relate to school employees.

Sixth, faculty meetings should be held at least monthly unless an emergency meeting is needed in the interim. I hold weekly administrative meetings to keep my administrators and myself informed and ahead of the "paper monster." Sometimes, though, the monster still eats me. Nevertheless, meetings between myself and instructional leaders are held every three weeks to ensure that the academic foci are kept before us as we strive to accomplish the objectives attached to them.

I put myself through a Reflection-Action-Reflection Cycle so that I can make the necessary changes in processes that thwart progress toward the school's vision. Remember—school impact leadership is specific curriculum practices being effectively and repetitively implemented at the schoolhouse. It is repetitive implementation of the practices that allows for systemic school improvement within a school district.

Once a school implements effective practices, it is only left to the district leadership (superintendents, assistant superintendents, etc.) to crystallize, standardize and create a process to ensure that all schools in the district are on the same page. School system leaders can get and stay on the "same page" by intentionally demonstrating the same behavior that evolves from an agreed upon philosophy. This does not mean all schools should be the same thematically, but there must be a streamlined philosophical structure and practice that all exhibit. Consequently, leaders should have a mantra that standardizes their thinking and keeps them stepping in the same direction.

In summary:

1. Prioritize your School Improvement Plan through the annual staff-training calendar.

2. Gauge under-developed skills and design differential training to meet individual needs.

3. Develop faculty and staff that can serve as role models for their colleagues.

4. Build departments and fortify areas of weakness.

5. Demonstrate MBWA: a proactive behavior that leads to academic excellence.

6. Conduct routine meetings with staff to keep focused.

7. Stay on top of the school's vision by the Reflection-Action-Reflection Cycle.

* * * * * * * * *

Unless we can extensively program our behavior, we waste tremendous amounts of information-processing capacity on trivia...
Alvin Toffler

What process can be used to standardize the practices of principals and curriculum leaders to ensure academic excellence throughout the district?

SYSTEMIC CHANGE PHILOSOPHY

Accomplishing the goal of even and consistent student academic achievement in urban school districts calls for systemic change. Nancy Boyd-Franklin says specific elements exist in any good system: for example stability, predictability, and identity. Thus, a good system that promotes student achievement will: *(1) consist of stable practices by adults with students; (2) render predicted results related to student and teacher behaviors in the educational process and; (3) allow academic results to have identifiable characteristics leaders can use as building blocks in the school improvement process.*

Principals and schoolhouse leaders can increase the possibility for student achievement if they think and behave systematically in the schools throughout the school district. In Peter Senge's book, *The Fifth Discipline*, he describes the idea of Systems Thinking as a language to help describe and understand the forces [i.e., effective staff practices with students] and interrelationships that shape the behavior in [educational] systems. In short, Systems Thinking entails a model of logical thought processes to a particular end.

For example, a traveler would find a current map to be a useful model which could help him get around more within cities and towns; in most cases, the traveler will reach his destination if fundamental behaviors are consistently demonstrated, such as reading the primary and secondary directions correctly—North, South, Northeast, Southwest, etc. He would also need to know how to read symbols that denote certain landmarks, i.e. churches, schools, etc.

The National Association of Secondary School Principals published in their report, *Breaking Ranks: Changing an American Institution,* that six logical landmarks, if effectively identified, could improve all schools. The professionals in this report state *personalization* should be a part of the school's environment. In other words, there should be a substantive and enabling relationship between students and teachers. *Coherency* should also be ensured.

Student requirements to graduate from high school should be clear, and curricula and testing should be appropriately aligned to ensure students' success. Again, this should be done from grade to grade. *Time* i.e. flexibility, is also presented as a construct to ensure student success. While flexibility is being proposed for high school students to obtain Carnegie Units, I believe this flexibility should be extended to students in earlier grades to help master essential concepts so that social promotions can become less tempting.

Obviously, *technology* can become an essential part of students' educational experiences given its inevitability in this society. The ever changing realities influencing education indicate the ongoing need for *professional development* for teachers and other adults working with students.

Finally, *leadership* is clearly needed to forge ahead to address the difficulties as a leader in an urban setting. These constructs help provide a framework in which principals and district leaders can focus to establish standardized practices to change urban education. Once there is a framework of sound constructs, an algorithm related to student academic achievement is needed for leaders to collectively execute.

Michael Goodman's proffers five steps in a Learning Model, for principals and leaders to model when focusing on systemic change and student academic achievement. This model consists of five key components: *(1) identify and collectively agree upon behaviors to be executed; (2) ensure that behaviors are replicated among colleagues; (3) meet to dialogue and readjust leadership behavior to the original focus; (4) leverage the success attained toward stated goals as a workable strategy for others; (5) continue new dialogues about other ways to attain chosen goals.*

This model, when agreed on and executed by principals standardizes leaders' behavior and increases the possibility of student academic achievement.

STANDARDIZING SCHOOL CLIMATE, STUDENT ATTENDANCE AND ACADEMIC ACHIEVEMENT

When school district principals agree to "get on the same page" in an effort to ensure a school climate that is conducive for learning, enforcing student attendance policies, monitoring student achievement, and creating and sharing strategies for parent involvement, progress is made immediately in the school district as well as in every area of focus.

I must insert here a caveat to schoolhouse and school district leaders. In many large urban school districts there are multiple issues regarding improvement that must be addressed. Thus, some leaders try to equally address them all. I strongly encourage these leaders to establish a primary, secondary, and tertiary focus and alternate between them. Leaders must know and understand the inner working of systems. Within systems one attribute is influenced by the other. As a matter of fact, when parts of a system break down, the other parts usually compensate for a period, albeit not as effectively.

Therefore, I encourage school district leaders to select the first, second, and third focus. If there are myriad focal points, I suggest you prioritize them in threes. The others will keep—don't worry. Leaders must invest their energy toward the primary focus. Be sure to include specific activities in your primary focus plan that will constantly contribute to the secondary and tertiary issues. In so doing, you build momentum and make progress from the primary focus to the others. Timely alternation from one focus to the other is essential. Thus, habits of maintenance must be developed by school leaders so they can continue to practice behavior that brings about improvement in the primary focal area. This process is doable at the district level and in the schoolhouse. Essential to this collective focus, however, is that principals must agree upon behaviors they will demonstrate to ensure success in focus areas aforementioned. Goodman's Learning Model can help principals maintain this focus.

It is crucial that principals' strategic focus come out of systematic dialogue. Dialogue sessions are essential because data shows that school progress is at varying levels of success. It would not be wise to have everyone focus on all data. It is essential, however, for principals to agree from the dialogue what the general focus will be. There must be a barometer that helps standardize and determine the level of focus.

The School Improvement Plan must be used to house the goals and activities to be executed. Once the focal areas have been established regarding school climate, student attendance, student achievement, and parent involvement, the activities created to achieve in these areas must serve as indicators that the principals will use to monitor themselves. It is important to say here that a standardized focus is difficult for principals to collectively engage if the school systems' goals are in flux because of constant leadership changes at the top of the school system organization.

Dialogue sessions among principals are significant to system progress. Professional team learning is a powerful process in school district improvement, and it must be taken seriously and acted upon by those in positions of authority. I believe a collective focus by principals will help to create a trend of success.

Betty Morgan, former Chief Academic Officer of Baltimore City Public School System, asserts that quality practices in schools over time with leaders having a clear vision and action for change will help induce academic progress. In a visual graphic, she depicts academic progress over time by showing an upward trend of instructional quality. She calls this a "Trend Bender."

Outlined below are goals and activities related to school climate, student attendance, academic achievement, and parental involvement. Suggested activities are given that I believe are essential in any school.

I do not, however, disregard the dialogue process that should happen between principals to determine what activities they will create and implement. However, I do believe that all principals will need to address school concerns related to these goals and activities at some point. Therefore, I present these goals and activities in general and request that principals focus in where there needs to be a dialogue. In some places on the outline, no activities are given. Thus, a dialogue and sharing session is needed to come up with substantive activities.

Goal: *The school environment will be conducive for learning.*

Activities:

1.   School leaders must create an environment of mutual respect: student to student, staff to student, and staff to staff.

2.   School leaders must establish consistent and clear rules and routines.

> A.   All students must have hall passes when moving through the building.
>
> B.   Progressive discipline is used with students in and out of the classroom.
>
> C.   Students are frequently and publicly praised for positive behaviors.
>
> D.   Detention is given as a consequence for misbehavior as opposed to suspension for some less severe behaviors.

E. Relationship building is used to establish good communication between students and teachers.

Goal: *Students' school attendance will be 90%.*

Activities:

1. School leaders will enforce the mandatory attendance policy for students; ten days or more absences from school will bring about a penalty. (Parents must be in this process)

   A. _____

   B. _____

2. School leaders will devise incentive programs to encourage school attendance. (Students must be in this process).

   A. _____

   B. _____

Goal: *Student achievement systems and state tests will be incremental but sustained.*

Activities:

1. School leaders must ensure that classroom instruction and assessments correlate with state tests/assessments.

2. School leaders must ensure they know the baseline data related to student achievement in their school.

3. School leaders must create a "Management by Walking Around" monitoring and feedback system to get effective consequences.

4. School leaders must have a strategy for remediating low performers in reading and math - preferably before or after school and on weekends.

5. School leaders must monitor instruction daily using:

    A. Documents that are used to check for curriculum pacing and other essential elements related to classroom instruction.

    B. Feedback process with teachers, both written and oral - monitoring the Performance Based Evaluation System (PBES) as required.

6. School leaders must inquire about student failure rate and plan strategies to decrease the same.

7. School leaders must identify "Test Impact Strategies" that positively effect state test data.

Goal: *Principals should share parent involvement strategies and activities with everyone who would benefit from hearing them.*

Activities:

1. _____

2. _____

Again, these goals and activities should only be implemented after a dialogue. The overall success of the student academic achievement process is contingent on a standard focus by principals on the four goals proposed above. Improvements in school climate, student attendance, and parent involvement will increase student academic achievement.

* * * * * * * * * *

Whatever affects one directly affects all indirectly.
I can never be what I ought to be until you are what you ought to be,
and you can never be what you ought to be until I am what I ought to be.
This is the interrelated structure of reality.
Martin Luther King, Jr.

PORTABLE CONCEPTS

- Curriculum leaders must prioritize the curriculum focus and execute it as planned.

- Adult staff must perceive and feel support from the administrators and their colleagues. Then they will likely support goals designed to increase academic achievement of students.

- Students will sustain engagement in the learning process when they believe that adults care enough about them to help them succeed.

- Teacher training and dialogue about goals and progress toward them are essential to student academic achievement.

CHAPTER SEVEN

STUDENT CONVERT MEETINGS

The art of persuasion has five chapters:
affirmation, repetition, prestige, suggestion, and contagion.

Erich Fromm

One morning I was sitting in the balcony of Bethel AME Church. Pastor Reid was bringing forth the Word and people were responding with "Amen," clapping and shouting. As I pondered how he was able to get such a response, my mind continuously revisited the themes about which he preached.

For example, he preached a sermon entitled, *"Living in the Ghetto But Not Having the Ghetto Live in You;"* and another sermon entitled, *"Raising Your Family in the Midst of Hell and Difficult Circumstances."* As I listened to these sermons I concluded that the "Word" could be used to reach students as long as it spoke to their reality; for this is what Pastor Reid does. I could not wait to get home to call my friend and colleague Roger Shaw, Principal of Paul Laurence Dunbar High School in Baltimore to share this new found insight. Roger is known to be very student centered, and I was confident that this new concept of Student Convert Meetings which was birthed out of me examining Pastor Reid's approach to preaching was indeed one Roger would use.

After changing out of my church attire and putting on more comfortable clothing, I called Roger. I discussed with him the idea that Student Convert Meetings are student assemblies which address issues related to student behaviors, and present excellent opportunities for school administrators to inspire students toward the vision of the school, while addressing topics related to their personal efforts, goals and mission.

The teacher (preacher) in the meetings must recognize the essential elements that should be a part of his/her presentation to students. The presentation should encompass a motivational and/or inspirational element. And it must also be reality based.

Pastor Reid of Baltimore's Bethel A.M.E. Church believes that people should not be beaten down from the pulpit by the message of the preacher. In other words, people should not merely be reminded of their faults. Rather, people should be inspired to move beyond their faults by accessing the power of God.

While teachers who inspire students must observe the law that separates church from state, inspiration must still be an objective in meetings. In Student Convert Meetings, the leader must always inspire students to make their best effort. I have found storytelling with students to be an excellent medium to motivate and inspire them.

Lest I am misunderstood, I do understand that inspiring our children – alone – is not enough. Presentations must connect directly the students' reality. Within this process, the speaker must talk about the painful realities that cause students to demonstrate attitudes and behaviors that are counter-productive, as well as acknowledge positive behaviors students demonstrate. Elements such as love and caring must be the overtone to these speeches or conversations. The following is the guide question for this chapter pertinent to Student Convert Meetings.

> **What topics can be effectively used with students in an urban environment to help them obtain and maintain productive behavior?**

SELF-ESTEEM VS.SELF CONCEPT

During Student Convert Meetings teachers can help students understand the difference between self-esteem and self-concept. I often share with students that self-esteem is how one feels about himself, while self-concept is how one sees himself. Students should be informed that they can see themselves (self-concept) as a good student and learn to feel good (self-esteem) about the same. On the other hand, students who have not met with success in school and who demonstrate negative behavior learn to see themselves as misbehaving students and unfortunately acquire good feelings about the same. This misbehavior is often reinforced by the constant response and attention to it.

Clarifying the information above for students can particularly help those whose behavior has been subtly conditioned within an environment that has planted negative self scripts which are stored in their heads.

SELECTIVE RESPECT

Students sometimes show particular adults a great deal of respect, while showing others no respect at all. As an administrator, I wondered why this was the case. After examining this phenomenon over a period of time and asking students about their behavior, I concluded that students believe they should respect adults who respect them. The notion of respect, however, was more than what it means at the surface level.

What students really mean when they speak of respect is that those teachers who cared about their feelings and circumstances, "deeply," were those who respected them and received their respect in return. Roger Shaw is emphatic that this is the case. He spends a great deal of time centering with students. He believes strongly that students select whom they are going to respect based on this meaning.

While speaking with students we must help them understand that some adults will go the extra mile to care and build a relationship with them while others won't. Students should be made to realize that every adult does not have to love or like them, but they should respect their human rights. Students must reciprocate this basic degree of respect. They do not have to love or like the adults with whom they interact, yet they must respect their human rights.

A MATTER OF PERCEPTION

People in general act and react based on the information they have accumulated while living in society. This information is then denoted as their reality. The realities students experience are stored in their minds as truths and untruths. So when adults interact with students, particularly to address misbehavior, students often believe in the behaviors they demonstrate based upon their reality. In other words, they see the behaviors from their perspective and their point of view.

To help students realize their perspective is just that – their perspective - administrators and teachers can use a glass of water that is filled to the middle. Ask students: "Is this glass half empty or half full?" After receiving the student's response, the adult should then present the other point of view. For example, if the student responds and says, "The glass is half full." And the teacher then says, "Its half empty," with a further explanation of why she sees the glass as half full, this strategy helps students to see that any given situation can be looked at two ways.

There is also a drawing used by those who assess individuals' personality or perception. The drawing has imbedded in it two pictures: one of an older lady and the other is a younger lady. Upon immediate viewing, some instantly recognize the older woman, while others see the younger lady. This drawing can also be used with students to reinforce the notion that people can view the same picture yet see two different things, thus have two different perspectives.

TEACHABLE MOMENTS

Administrators and teachers can use incidents in the school to point out the flaws or lack of reflection in students' thinking as a way of making a point to students.

For example, eight students were once in a room. The fire alarm in the room was set off, yet none of the students did it. Each of them emphatically denied pulling the alarm. "It must have been a ghost," I said. The teachable moment here is that when you are lying, the truth will "make you free."

Teachable moments jolt reflection, dialogue and action on the behalf of the student(s)—considering the information provided by the teacher. The information given by the teacher figuratively boxes the student into a position wherein he's almost forced to acknowledge the circumstances before him.

For example, in the case of the pulled false alarm, the teacher (principal) responds to students by saying, "Take out a sheet of paper. You will have a mandatory pop quiz. Here is the assignment: Explain the following: (the principal writes on the chalkboard) A fire alarm was pulled in this classroom. The alarm bell rang. The pulled station was clearly activated in this room where there are fifty of you. All of you stated, "It wasn't me!" Describe five ways on your paper that that false alarm could have happened in this room—given that none of you pulled it. Your answers in this assignment will be checked by me and the Baltimore City Fire Marshal. Oh, by the way, the fine for false alarm is $5,000 or imprisonment.

The teachable moment is as the title implies – to teach.

WELFARE

For some students in Urban America, the idea of receiving public assistance or "being on welfare," as some students would say, brings shame to those in this predicament. Educators should realize this and appropriately address the issue. Students who are dependent upon adults who are dependent upon welfare must be informed that receiving public assistance has no disabling effect on reaching their goals and dreams. As a matter of fact, students must be encouraged to break the cycle of welfare dependency by doing well in school and ultimately securing a job or business career. Welfare for children is an inherited status that must be viewed as a predicament that can be changed. I often tell my students that "they should not be occupied with being on welfare, but they should concentrate and be certain that they are fairing well in all endeavors.

UNIFORMS FOR UNIFORMITY

Walbrook High School Uniform Services Academy was the first public high school in Baltimore City where one hundred percent of the students wore uniforms. As you might have guessed, getting students to wear uniforms was no easy task. In fact, the idea of wearing uniforms actually "cramped the students' style."

Therefore, a great sales job during meetings was necessary in order to persuade fifteen hundred students to wear uniforms. I sold the idea of safety, uniformity, and unity. These three ideas are interconnected. Students were informed that when we all are in uniform, outsiders or intruders would not be able to infiltrate our school, and as a result safety would be maintained.

The notion of school uniformity relative to school uniforms was an observable reference point that allowed the adults to encourage unity in various aspects of the school program. Overall, school uniforms can contribute positively to school climate.

COMMON LANGUAGE & METAPHORS

Throughout the book, I have mentioned that it is essential to emphasize critical ideas such as vision, mission, rules, policies, etc. I have also emphasized that you want people to attend to, internalize, and effectively act upon these ideas. I have found that having staff and students speak in "one voice" positively contributes to the goals of the school. This process becomes easier when staff throughout the building uses a common language.

I also discovered that metaphors are useful with students. I observed how they focused and gave meaning to the events and ideas in their environment. Thus, I adopted the same methods students used by giving meaning to events and ideas to which I wanted them to pay attention. And it worked! So, in the Student Convert Meetings as well as in other places in the schoolhouse I encourage my staff to use the following language to address students' behavior: *Puppet vs. Puppeteer; Keeping the Juice; Space & Face Rule; Nerds Get Paid.*

PUPPET VS. PUPPETEER

Too many students are bombarded with negative images of attaining money, power, and respect. Often these images are presented to the detriment of children who do not have responsible guidance to help them interpret the reality in relationship to the images.

The image of money is presented in the context where it is attained by selling drugs, playing sports (usually football, baseball, and basketball) and/or entertaining as rap artists. In these endeavors, students seek again money, power, and respect. Conversely, students, however, are rarely bombarded with images that encourage them to delay gratification for future goals. Therefore, I thought it was important to introduce students to the Puppet/Puppeteer metaphor.

The essence of the lesson is to help students establish power and control over self that will lead to self-respect as well as respect from others. Students are encouraged to be the puppeteer and not the puppet.

187

The puppeteer is the controller of the strings. The puppet moves at the puppeteers command. Students want to feel that they are in control of their actions. Therefore, adults should show students how they are allowing their peers to anger, persuade, and control them. Students must be taught to be puppeteers who are in control of their behavior.

As an aside, it is important to note that the behavior in the school environment must support puppeteer behavior as being the rule. In other words, puppeteers must become the icons to be admired. In order for this and all metaphors to become pervasive school-wide, all staff must use the language. The puppeteer has the juice. The juice is equivalent to the puppeteer. When the student has the juice, she has the power or control. These metaphors have had great power and usefulness for students in our school.

SPACE and FACE RULE

Many students I have taught have told me that their parents have stated relative to disputes, "If they hit you, hit them back." Students shared this information with me during conferences when I met with them to establish the cause of a fight. After hearing the idea repeatedly during many conferences, this was seemingly the only strategy students brought to a dispute. I then felt compelled to provide them with information that would help them *prevent* the fight. Thus the Space and Face Rule was established.

We told students if the student they were "beefing with" (disputing with) was not in their space and face, they had the opportunity to avoid the problem. In instances where students were approached, we encouraged them to back away. Only spontaneous self-defense would not make a student liable for the fight. Spontaneous self-defense entails an individual being suddenly confronted or bodily threatened.

At all cost, we encourage students to use the Space and Face Rule. We also encourage students not to approach other students given second hand information without a responsible adult mediator, because they could not control how the other student would respond. The bottom line: "If they are not in your space and in your face, they are no threat to you at that time. Therefore, try to resolve the issue with a responsible mediator."

NERDS GET PAID

For many teenagers in urban school systems it is becoming more and more difficult to focus on education as a life priority. Many of these teenagers, unfortunately, are seeing fewer family members use education as a tool of upward mobility in the American society. Thus educational competence is not trendy to urban youth. Students believe it is not cool to be smart. Typically, if you are smart you could be and sometimes are considered "a nerd."

When meeting with students, it is essential to debunk the idea that those who study are in fact nerds. This idea is debunked by poignantly articulating that nerds are those who read, write, compute, get jobs and eventually get paid! The bottom line is that students must know that it is not only cool to be smart, but it's also potentially profitable to be smart.

The four metaphors presented above are just some of that which my staff and I created as a common language. There is power in using metaphors. The key to the metaphors is that they are reality-based. In other words, adults must listen to the meanings that students make. Once we understand these made meanings, we will be able to help guide our students more effectively during their developmental process.

THE FORMULA FOR SUCCESS

Listening to conversations and observing behaviors of many students gives me a chance to hear them articulate and demonstrate their disbelief about attaining opportunities to which they are exposed by the staff. It seems as if our students lose faith that goals and opportunities are attainable because no one ensures their dreams in the interim and there is no information given to them regarding how goals come to fruition.

The interim regarding students' dreams and goals is the time after students establish beliefs before goals would have come to fruition had they pursued them. It is because of interim periods in students' lives that Student Convert Meetings are necessary. Student Convert Meetings are held to help our students sustain their hopes about their goals and redefine their thinking after hearing needed information. We also use these settings to clarify for students how others become successful by sharing with them the success formula as proposed by Tony Robbins, which entails:

- Finding or identifying a "successful" person
- Observing what they do
- Doing what they do.

In addition, we share with students that they can "Backward Map" a successful person's life. In other words, start with where a person is presently in their career, go backward two years at time, and pinpoint what preparation behaviors were being demonstrated in route to where they are presently in their career.

The formula for success must be shared with students so that their future goals are coupled with a strategy to reach them. The preaching, teaching, and reaching that take place in student Convert Meetings are an essential element in the educational process and seem to be that which students need. I have personally seen students thoroughly enjoy the encouragement that takes place in the meetings.

MAN IN THE MIRROR

Working with students during the educational process, I discovered that students took credit for behaviors that they and others perceived to be good or cool. Conversely, students blamed others when they fell short of an expectation that was clear or attainable. Often, students assigned blame to something or someone outside of them when they were caught breaking a school rule. My interpretation of this behavior was that students had learned to be irresponsible. They were not taught to own their failures or shortcomings by blaming someone else for their misbehavior. Essentially, they presented themselves as the victim when in fact they were the perpetrator or initiator.

While sitting in my office one day at Greenspring Middle School I thought about how one of my former principals placed mirrors in the hallways so students could admire themselves. Thus I realized that having mirrors placed on walls was not a farfetched idea. However, it was my intent to use the mirrors to help students address both the "blaming" and "victim" behaviors.

During the disciplinary process, students would in many cases blame others for their circumstances. When this occurred, I asked the students to go to the mirror, and I would give them the following instructions: "Prepare to tell me about you and your involvement in this situation." I would ask students what they could have done differently. The mirror was also used in the progressive discipline process. Students were sent to the mirror to reflect on their behavior for a designated period.

To address the victim behavior, students were told that the person they saw in the mirror was responsible for 90% of what happened to them. They were also told that they were in charge of their destiny.

POST TRAUMATIC SLAVE SYNDROME

One morning I was listening to a sermon being delivered by Pastor Frank Reid. He referenced a study being done by a doctoral student somewhere on the East Coast of the United States. He stated that the scholar of this particular research asserted a parallel between Post Traumatic Stress Disorder (PTSD) and Post Traumatic Slave Syndrome (PTSS).

PTSD is a mental disorder occurring after a traumatic event. I also believe there are lingering effects from slavery for those of African descent in America who have not participated in physical, intellectual, emotional, spiritual, and social sessions of therapeutic value. PTSS, on the other hand, manifests itself as self-hate, discouraging recollections, and familial/cultural detachment.

In Student Convert Meetings, I often find myself attempting to inform students by referencing ideas I established by reading and understanding the psychocultural effects of African Slavery in this country. Frequently, I found myself talking to all students in the meeting, but young boys in particular, who have been incarcerated, or those who might be eventually on their way because they break the law but have not been caught yet.

The Post Traumatic Slave Syndrome idea leads me to parallel for students the relationship between the slave and the slave master on the plantation or in jail. Students are informed that the slave could not come and go as he pleased just as they can't once they are incarcerated.

This lack of freedom idea is expounded upon relative to not seeing loved ones when the slave/inmate chooses and not eating when the slave/inmate wants to eat, etc. I also tell students that they have the *maroon* within them in the manner that Asa Hilliard explains in his book, *The Maroon Within Us.*

The Maroons were Africans who were enslaved but fought nonetheless for their freedom. I share with students that a solid and proper education will provide their freedom in this country and treat (PTSS). There are many other ideas I use to inform students which are generated from the affects of slavery. The aforementioned are just a few.

MEAN STREETS OF MAINSTREAM

NAACP President and CEO, Kweisi Mfume, wrote the book entitled, *No Free Ride: Mean Streets to Mainstream.* In this book references are made about how Mr. Mfume worked through trials and tribulations he faced while growing up in an urban environment. I submit that most urban youth face obstacles and tribulations growing up in the inner city across this country. I also contend that many urban youth who yearn to work and participate in society's "mainstream" eventually adjust behaviors and attitudes that were shaped by the environment from which they come. Therefore, I spend my time talking to students about being assertive vs. being aggressive.

Assertive behavior has all of the energy as aggressive behavior, but no one is intentionally offended as one moves to accomplish a particular task. Aggressive behavior entails striving to accomplish a particular task regardless of whether or not someone is offended in the process. Often offensive behavior is *one's modus operandus* when he is being aggressive.

Finally, I have also discussed with students the need to speak both slang and proper English at the appropriate time. I call it being "bilingual." Being able to speak mainstream English is important. I have often found myself discussing with students the need to adjust their behavior while making the transition from the mean streets to mainstream. Roger and I have also discussed all of these topics on one occasion or another.

Giving students information that can directly affect and positively change their lives is essential. My colleague and I believe that Student Convert Meetings are an excellent forum by which to make this happen.

* * * * * * * * *

One of the best ways to persuade
others is with your ears—by listening to them.
Dean Rusk

PORTABLE CONCEPTS

- Students need a periodic word of encouragement.
- Students can be persuaded to change if information shared with them speaks to their circumstances and reality.
- Leaders in urban schools must understand the psycho-cultural reality of students to effectively work with them and provide appropriate guidance.

CHAPTER EIGHT

THE DILEMMA AND
THE CHALLENGE

Where there is no struggle; there is no freedom.
Power concedes nothing without demand; it never did and it never will.
Frederick Douglas

Within the writings and speeches of Dr. Martin Luther King Jr., he often discussed the dilemma encountered by people participating in the struggle for justice. Whether having to decide to risk losing a job by choosing not to use public transportation in Montgomery, Alabama or adhering to the pledge of non-violent resistance in the midst of being beaten by police during a peaceful demonstration, Dr. King discussed with the people the perplexity and pride involved in bringing about justice. He also referenced the challenges in securing justice and freedom in the midst of social injustice and bondage.

The challenge for those seeking freedom and justice entailed steadfastness and clarity of purpose. Dr. King encouraged freedom fighters not to tire, but to have peace that passed the understanding of those who participated in unjust acts. History reports in discussions in peace meetings, Dr. King encouraged participants of the civil rights struggle to: "Envy not the oppressor, and choose none of his ways."

This scripture not only has within it the power to guide those participating in the civil rights struggle, it has application for adults who participate in the struggle to liberate the minds of students who live in poverty and attend urban schools across this nation. Clearly, these students should be encouraged not to take on the ways and mannerisms of those who participate in their personal and or social oppression.

Students from urban environments have, unfortunately, limitless opportunities to envy the oppressor and act in a like manner. Thus the dilemma for many students is who will help them grapple with the immensity of those issues that are an outgrowth of oppression in an effort to steer clear of adopting those same oppressive behaviors themselves.

Having said this, the additional challenge for students is to establish a plan to improve their life's quality by garnering support from others to help them execute the plan.

The guide question then for this chapter is as follows:

HOW DO PRINCIPALS HELP STUDENTS RESPOND TO DILEMMAS AND CHALLENGES THAT DISTRACT THEM IN THE EDUCATIONAL PROCESS?

As we attempt to answer this question, we do so by sharing with you a series of stories that clearly depict the need for principals to help students respond to dilemmas and challenges that distract them in the educational process. The stories shared in this chapter are real, however, the names, roles, some particulars have been changed or deleted to protect the confidentiality of those involved. The gist of these stories have been maintained so that those with an interest in improving the quality of life of students in urban education will know the true nature of the challenge. Solutions for these problems will be left to you as you fathom the enormity and depth of issues that oppressed children face.

The holistic community movement idea toward the end of the chapter serves as a framework of strategies that the committed can use to take action and help children face challenges and surmount obstacles.

Story 1: THEY SUPPOSED TO BE MY FRIENDS

One spring semester, my executive assistant called me away from the office. She said, *"I think you should come to my office to talk to this student."* When I entered her office, Terry was crying incessantly. I inquired, *"Terry! Terry! What's wrong sweetie?"* She continued to cry. So, I just put my arm around her shoulder and sat beside her. I said to her, *"Whatever it is, precious it'll be alright."* Then Terry began to state, *"Doc"* (which is the abbreviated address for Dr. Bundley), *they suppose to be my friends!"* I then asked, *"What happened?"* She began telling me that, *"My mother is out there,"* (which meant her mother was addicted to crack cocaine. I learned this by listening and asking questions during our conversation). Still, I was somewhat confused because my mind returned to her earlier statement - "They supposed to be my friends." She seemed to have calmed down some. I asked again, *"What's the matter?"* She responded, *"They hurt me so bad, Dr. Bundley."* *"Who hurt you Terry?"* She began telling me. *"I came back into my house from the store, and she was sucking my friends_____."* (Terry was speaking of her mother.) *"They suppose to be my friends, and they walking around telling everybody. I can't stay at this school, Doc."*

While Terry was telling me about her experience, I was crying inside. I held back the tears, hoping to be strong for her. I did manage to get Terry to another school. I pray often that Terry is doing okay.

The **dilemma** is that many people (parents of students) are waiting for America to win the propagandized war on drugs so they can only have their addictions to attend to without worrying about having access to the same drug that has them preoccupied with their addiction. The **challenge** is that there is no war on drugs and the lives of many students have been deeply affected because of the drug epidemic. As educators, we are charged with distilling waters of life, using the educational process, so that students will have a chance to lead productive lives.

Educators in this new millennium must be mindful that the drug epidemic will impact negatively on the educational mission. Therefore, proactive practices must be administered accordingly.

Story 2: I WANT TO GO TO COLLEGE

I was comfortably nestled in my office, rearranging the mounds of paper that hid the fruit wood finish on my Victorian style desk. Then, without any warning, my calm was interrupted. *"You better get the f_____ off of me,"* is the statement I vaguely heard behind the closed doors in my office. I got up from the desk and came into the outer office. There, Walther yelled, *"Dr. Bundley, you better tell them to keep their f____ hands off of me."* I asked Walther to calm down and invited him and the two adults who were escorting him into the office.

Once we were behind closed doors, I sought to gain information about the matter. As I usually do, I asked the student to explain what happened. After his explanation, the two adults concurred with his version of the story. The gist of the story is that Walther and another student were arguing in class. The teacher asked both to desist. The other student stopped. Walther continued. He was asked to leave the classroom. Initially, he wouldn't. Then Walther got out of his seat, moved toward the student with whom he was arguing, and the teacher intervened. Walther began yelling profanities. The teacher from next door stepped into the room where there was commotion. They both guided Walther to my office.

After allowing Walther to calm down, I thanked the two teachers for escorting him and they left. Walther remained and I stated, *"Walther, given what you have shared with me, how did the situation escalate to screaming, cursing, escorts, etc.?"* He just sat there quietly for a moment. Then he stated, *"Me and the boy were just playing at first."* I asked Walther again, *"Why did it lead to yelling and cursing?"* *"I just got mad*

Dr. Bundley", he stated. *"Dr. Bundley, for real, they are getting ready to move me again."* (He was referring to employees from the Department of Social Services.) Walther assumed that I knew he was in foster care. He further stated, *"They gettin on my nerves."*

I began asking Walther questions about his background. He told me that his mother died of AIDS and his father was incarcerated. I hoped to encourage by saying, *"There will always be people willing to help you, if you help yourself."* He responded, *"Dr. Bundley, I want to go to college and make something out of my life. I don't want to be out there in them streets."*

At that moment I made up my mind to be one of those willing to help Walther if he helped himself. He is now doing well. I anticipate he will graduate in the spring. He stated to me during one of our daily conversations: *"Dr. Bundley, did you know that foster care children can go to college free in the state of Maryland?"* *"No, I didn't,"* I responded. *"I'm goin to college,"* shouted Walther! And with the same jubilation as Walther - unrestricted and irrefutable - I replied, *"I know that's right!"*

I pray for Walther's success.

The **dilemma** is the increase in the number of foster care children throughout this country. The **challenge** is to create and establish school environments to appropriately address students who manifest behaviors that are indicative of students being separated from biological parents—often for reasons beyond their control. Charter schools will not solve the problem given the pain, neglect, and abuse manifested by many students, including those in foster care. Only a programmatic paradigm shift by educators will suffice. Where there is pain students need hope, i.e. a future orientation, because the past and present life experiences seem to dim all possibilities.

Story 3:
DOC, YOU DON'T KNOW US

One day while walking through the courtyard during a lunch period three female students spoke to me. I responded, *"Hi ladies."* One of the students said, *"Dr. Bundley, you don't know us. We are your honor roll students, and you don't even know our names."* I immediately stopped and asked each one of them their name.

Patrice, I discovered was the most vocal who stated, *"You know the names of all those bad children, but you don't know the names of us who do the things you say."* I thought about what Patrice stated in that moment and her observation stays with me even today.

I learned by listening to these students that if adults do not take time to learn the names of those who are and should be the role models in the school, we will spend a great deal of time unintentionally ignoring them by dealing with students who misbehave. This, of course, must not occur. Administrators must make it our business to intentionally get to know those who serve as paragons in the school.

The **dilemma** is the lack of knowledge that many educators, politicians, and critical observers of public education have about the fact that there is only a minority of children who create the problems for the majority in schools in urban environments across this country. Yet a penumbra of doubt and aspersion is usually cast on all students in urban schools further eroding the confidence of those who only have public education as an option. The **challenge** is to get all who suggest that they care to converge, collectively, on the schools and participate to make them better. A critical mass of troubled students who are noticed by constant misbehavior can preoccupy teachers and administrators to the point where model students are unfortunately ignored; when in reality they ought to be celebrated daily.

Story 4:
Sir, Why Don't You Stop?

While returning to Baltimore from a very important conference, I received a page from an assistant principal. He asked if I was sitting down. I responded by telling him, *"I'm on the train, so yes I'm sitting down."* He went on to say: *"Ms. Allen was hit in the head with a ____ by a student."* With my heart, now in my stomach, I asked, *"What happened?"* He proceeded to tell me what happened. After listening to him, here is my understanding of what he stated.

Ms. Allen would not allow Tonya into the classroom because she did not have her notebook. As Ms. Allen stood in the door to direct Tonya to the office, Tonya attempted to push past Ms. Allen, almost knocking her down. The assistant principal then intervened. Ms. Allen requested to see Tonya's parent as opposed to having her suspended for assault. The assistant principal honored Ms. Allen's request by sending Tonya home for a specified time and requiring that she bring her parent back to school at a specified time.

Before Tonya was to return to school, she came into the building. Ms. Allen saw Tonya and asked if she was with a parent. Tonya became verbally abusive so Ms. Allen called for the assistant principal to inquire about Tonya's presence in the building. The assistant principal retrieved Tonya and asked her why she was in the building without a parent and called the parent to come to the school to address the situation. When

Tonya's parent arrived at the school, he was sent to the assistant principal's office where Tonya was already sitting alone.

Because the assistant principal had to attend to other school matters, Tonya and her father walked out of the office and down the hallway while waiting. While in the hallway a yelling match ensued between Tonya and her father. A teacher walked into the hallway during the profane yelling between the father and child. Suddenly, the father physically accosted Tonya. Then, Ms. Jones (the teacher who was now witnessing the incident) stated, *"Sir, why don't you stop treating that child in such manner."* By that time the assistant principal had returned to his office where Ms. Allen was waiting for him. He invited Ms. Allen into the office and shortly thereafter Tonya and her dad entered the office suite and were invited in as well. The meeting was commenced by the assistant principal when he asked Ms. Allen to share with the parent why she requested the conference. Shortly after Ms. Allen began providing information, Tonya's father interjected.

The gist of his comments centered on the idea of the school personnel being unfair toward Tonya. When the assistant principal asked the father to be fair in the conference by allowing Ms. Allen to finish her comments, the father insisted upon dominating the conference periodically using profane language. The assistant principal finally interjected saying: *"If you do not allow the conference to take place in an orderly and respectful manner then it is over."* The parent continued in the same vain. The assistant principal terminated the conference. Tonya then stated, *"If it wasn't for my father and the way he acted, you would have let me stay."* The assistant principal looked at Tonya with a nod of concurrence. Then he looked to Ms. Allen and stated, *"You can return to your class."* Ms. Allen exited the assistant principal's office. Seconds later, Tonya calmly got out of her chair and proceeded in the same direction as Ms. Allen. From the account given by the secretary, Tonya picked up the stapler from her desk and hit Ms. Allen in the head with the stapler stating angrily, *"I don't give a f__k now!"* Ms. Allen, head dripping with blood tried to regain her mental faculties, fighting off Tonya she thought, who was actually not there because she had run out of the building being urged by her father.

> The **dilemma** is that the generation gap is drastically being decreased. More teenagers are having children, reducing family generations to fifteen years and unfortunately even less in some situations. Teenagers who have babies often lack crucial parenting skills because they are busy being teenagers after the babies are born. Meanwhile, the children's behaviors are being shaped by the environmental influences where they reside. The **challenge** is, first, to relieve grandmothers in many urban settings across this country from their duties of being mothers for the second time around, while thanking them for "standing in the gap" in the meantime. Simultaneously parenting programs should be offered to some parents and mandated for others while the education owed to their children is rendered.

Story 5: MY MOTHER IS REALLY UPSET WITH ME...

During winter break, one of my colleagues took time out of his hectic schedule to call me. He served as a principal at one of the high schools in the city. As our conversation often goes, we began talking about educational issues. He told me about a situation that he said touched his heart and confirmed for him again the reality of the difficult life experiences our students go through.

My colleague described to me how a teacher sent a student to the office on numerous occasions for sleeping in the classroom. He described how he had to intervene on a situation where the student became hostile with the teacher and stated to her, *"You don't know sh__."* It was this comment by the student that led my colleague to ask the student, *"What is it that the teacher doesn't know?"* The student with a rivulet of tears on his cheek stated to my colleague: *"My mother is really upset with me because I am bisexual. That's why I sleep in class. I really don't stay with my mother all of the time because she stays on my nerves. So, I just stay over different friends houses and I don't get any sleep."* I asked my colleague what was his response. He said, *"Man, I didn't know what to say at first."* Then he stated that he asked the student what he planned to do about his situation, to which the student responded, *"I don't know. You know Mr.____, I have grown up watching my mother and her lesbian friends all my life. I don't know why my mother tripping."*

I am seeing more homosexual children than ever before. I would be hesitant to write this statement in such a pronounced way if it were not for the large number of male and female students who do not hide the fact that they are homosexual. It is to my dismay when I discover in conversations with students some of the known abuses, homosexual in nature, they have experienced in their young lives. The **dilemma** is while some students have chosen homosexual lifestyles; others who have a history of sexual abuse fight with all their heart to behave in the manner that is in consonance with their gender. The manifestation of this personality struggle shows up in ways where counseling and guidance are necessary. The **challenge** is for educators to realize homosexual students are ours to educate. There is a need to discuss how adults can maintain a school environment that respects and proves sensitive to students who have been sexually abused; some of whom have homosexual lifestyles.

These are stories of our babies ... our children, those who are students in our schools. From the manner in which many bureaucrats proceed to educate in urban America, you would think that many in school bureaucracies are clueless about the realities educators experience in schools, daily. There is this chasm between the bureaucracy and the community/school. Some in the bureaucracy might be offended by my assertion that they are clueless. But, I have no other conclusion to which to come after observing the philosophy and practice of urban school officials across the nation.

What seems to be common in many urban school districts is the notion that principals, teachers, faculty, etc. will bring about success of students to reach state standards that seem, in the minds of students, irrelevant to the realities they live everyday. There are few to no policies or processes that connect education to psychological and cultural realities that students and parents live daily. Education, if it is to be effectively engaged by urban students and their families, must directly show how the quality of life for them will improve by engaging in the educational process. Thus, I endorse the community engagement strategy proposed by the Hare family.

Drs. Nathan and Julia Hare propose a strategy that will promote a people's movement to help students in their schools. They state effective practice for urban students entails both centrifugal and centripetal activities on the part of concerned adults. In other words, school officials must establish programs within the school that create a positive force that prepare students to be effective in community and society, while creating community structures external to the school that directly influence the success of accomplishing educational standards established for students.

Programs and activities external to the school should be designed to address the needs and concerns of the community members, particularly the adults who have school age children. It is not wise, however, to allow community programs with similar purposes to operate separately and apart from each other. Programs which are allowed to operate separately when it is obvious that they serve the same purpose invite dissension and missed opportunities to be collectively effective in helping members of the community.

Dissension is sewn between programs with similar purpose by those who have been taught the selfish – "I" mentality. This kind of thinking connotes individuals who look at projects of service and ask: "What can I get out of this?" and "How can my establishment be first?" This kind of selfish thinking is detrimental to establishing a collective community consciousness essential for helping parents help their children in school.

When individuals who work in separate programs with similar purposes do not organize to work together, they make themselves vulnerable to those who would see to sow discord. Those who seek to divide individuals usually use strategies that entail:

- Dividing minimal amounts of money to too many groups with the same purpose under the guise of healthy competition.
- Spreading negative propaganda and manipulating competitive organizations for the act of it.

To decrease the opportunity for discord between organizations, a coordinating action can be initiated to bring organizational programs together to create a movement that includes all concerned people in the community. Organizations with similar missions must collaborate in their area of expertise. When coordinators get varied groups of experts to work collectively in their specific fields, then one can say the onset of a Community Movement has begun. Essential fields of experts who can contribute to success of school age children in urban America are those who:

- Create opportunities for economic development;
- Observe and contribute ideas toward proper education for urban students;
- Provide support and societal reintegration strategies for ex-offenders;
- Provide information and strategies of recovery to those who are substance abusers;
- Educate and enlighten members in the community about the political process;
- Seek support for the homeless population;
- Engage the police and law "enforcement" officials in the process of community support;
- Network families in communities to be a family force on issues;
- Encourage members of the faith-based organization to participate in strategies of community building.

Synchronized and massive movement of experts in the fields aforementioned will contribute to students' success in schools. The dilemma lies within those who ignore and suppress the part of their conscience that reminds them of their obligation to help improve the quality of life for children.

The challenge is to pique conscience of the same people by speaking the historical and plain truth about how and why our children have been subjected to these conditions. The Bible serves to help us at this point as Deuteronomy 4:9 states: *"Only guard yourself and guard your soul carefully. Lest you forget the things your eyes saw. And lest these things depart your heart all the days of your life and ye shall make them known to your children and your children's children."*

The Sunday I finished this chapter I listened to a sermon by my former pastor, Dr. Reid, titled, *"You Can Overcome the Fear Factor: Stay Focused."* A crucial point in his sermon was that one needed constant faith to stay focused. I believe faith was the element that kept Dr. King focused during the dilemmas and challenges of the 1960s. I also believe this same faith is going to be needed by people who are experiencing the changing and sometimes, unrecognizable face of urban education.

The goodness and potential in the children are still evident. It only takes those with faith to know that negativity must shrink to positivism—just as Satan must yield to God. Those people of faith must say no thank you to people who try to lend them their lens that only shows the gloomy point of view that urban education and everything and everybody in it are failing miserably.

Intelligent people realize that every cause has an effect that can eventually be traced to another cause. Thus the misdeeds of urban education, however gloomy they may have become, are not to be totally blamed on those waiting to be educated. The students are actors in the educational environment, not progenitors of it. Victor Hugo states it this way: "*Wherever there is darkness, sins will be committed. But he who is guilty is not only he who committed the sin, but he who created the darkness.*"

Concern and committed educators shine light where there is darkness by having faith to bring about effective practices, even if they appear to be "out of the box" with the thinking and actions of many. The important thing is that they are ethical and address the educational dilemma and meet the challenges faced. I believe the only way urban schools will be restored on the inside is by massive movement by the community stakeholders from the outside.

* * * * * * * * * *

We are troubled on every side, yet not distressed;
we are perplexed but not in despair; persecuted,
but not forsaken; cast down, but not destroyed.
2 Corinthians 4:8-9

PORTABLE CONCEPTS

- Effective programs, however untraditional, have to be designed to address the dilemmas and challenges students face.

- Educators should be people who maintain confidence in the midst of adversity in order to help students do the same.
- Massive community movements that help improve the quality of life of residents will inevitably improve the effective actions of students in schools.

CHAPTER NINE

FINAL THOUGHTS

Education is an element in the struggle for human rights.
It is the means to help our children and people rediscover their identity
and thereby increase self-respect. Education is the passport to our future.
Tomorrow belongs to those who prepare today.

Malcolm X

As I reflect on my state of being when I started writing this book, I am able to recapture the growing confidence and the elation I felt. Students' lives were being positively changed because I dared to challenge the status quo, disturb the institutional equilibrium of non-expectancy, and embrace sound educational practices; practices perceived by many as "out of the box" thinking and action. But in all actuality, with great humility, the practices I implemented were headlong reaches to save drowning children – *our babies*! And though at times I am accused of unconventional wisdom; censured by comfortable obsolete bureaucrats who find my well-meaning objectives obscure, I have taken great lengths to secure these, my final thoughts, simplistic and rather mainstream. They are essential and contribute significantly to my ideas in educating the urban child.

STUDENT LEADERSHIP

One of the most difficult tasks I have experienced as an urban administrator is getting parents to collectively support the educational process in the school. I believe that parents are a child's first teacher. Although most students eventually attend school outside of the home, parents still play an integral part in the educational process.

Regardless of the socio-economic status, parent involvement is usually evident in the early grades. This involvement gradually decreases as students move from early grades toward high school. The trend demonstrates that students who have parents attend college show a similar interest in furthering their education after high school. Thus, those students whose parents are college completers usually, at the least, are inspired by their parents to complete high school. There are instances, however, where parents who only complete high school have students do the same, and some students even go beyond their parents to attend college.

Whatever the case, there are still too many students not graduating high school because of the lack of student focus and parental guidance. We can ill afford to use the excuse that the absence of parent involvement results in student failure in urban schools. Effective programming, as a matter fact, must be developed to fill the void where parent support is lacking. Thus, I believe a strategy that gets students involved in promoting their own development is a viable strategy. This student development strategy is entitled Student Leadership.

The process of student leadership starts with students' input regarding how to improve their school. Essential to this process is adult support of the students. Students in the school must believe that they have the support of the staff when it comes to helping them face issues inside and outside of school. Other students must perceive students who participate in establishing criteria for school clubs and taking on leadership roles as those who are positive leaders.

Throughout the nation's public school systems, the student-teacher ratio is overwhelming. Students will forever outnumber teachers and adults in most learning institutions. Nonetheless, in urban schools, it is essential that programs of interest be established for students. These programs must foster the idea of leadership as the core philosophy that students must commit themselves.

Student leadership can be a major contributing factor in creating and maintaining a positive school culture. School culture is defined as the ethos or underlying and guiding beliefs of the students and adults as a collective. The school climate is the visible activities in the school, some of which grow out of school culture. When student leadership is evident, incidents and activities, which occur away from adult supervision, are appropriately handled by students. Student leaders feel compelled because of their self-concept and self-esteem to protect the values that make up the culture of the school.

It is advantageous for adults to systematically make all students in the school realize that they too have an opportunity to be a student leader. First of all, urban schools must have enough clubs and activities to accommodate the entire student body. Adults should solicit ideas and suggestions from students regarding the types of clubs and activities they want in their school. It is important to always include the very people in the planning process who are most affected by its outcome. Once the clubs and activities are established, staff members should continually encourage students to exhibit exemplary behavior while participating. As students demonstrate positive and noteworthy behavior, they should be publicly recognized. I have often heard educators say, "What's inspected becomes expected."

Regarding student recognition for positive behavior, once students realize that you view particular behavior as extraordinary and publicly recognize it, students begin to expect your acknowledgement whenever they demonstrate such noteworthy behavior. I have seen this type of student expectation ripple and positively contribute to the overall school climate.

Student leaders can help shape the behaviors of students transferring from other schools. This is a delicate process and requires expertise on the part of adults to ensure that student leaders appropriately assist in shaping new attitudes and behaviors of other students. Adults must make certain that student roles are clearly defined and that students operate within them.

For example, we devised a strategy at Greenspring Middle where students transferring to the school, or entering from suspension, went through an interview process. During the process, student leaders and adult facilitators queried students about topics that indirectly related to the core values (character) of the school. The purpose of the interview was to initially gauge the student's attitude and possibly surmise and prepare for the "transition behavior" in school – good or ill-tempered. Administrators were permitted to deny or accept the enrollment or return of a student based on recommendations from the interview panel. It was also essential that students were protected from any reprisals sought by students who resented them for being "on the school's side." You'll find in some cases, students who have not experienced success or engaged the school positively show resentment toward the students who choose to do the right thing. Consequently, it is essential for the administrative staff to detect any signs of this and address it immediately and effectively.

Student leadership is essential in the school. When students help create a positive school culture, the values therein are recognized faster by the student body. Student behavior is more readily influenced through other students. Thus, having them serve as positive role models for each other is an asset for the climate. It only becomes the adult's responsibility, then, to articulate the vision and mission of the school and inspire students toward it.

CREATING NEW TRADITIONS

Some social scientists present the unproductive behaviors demonstrated in the urban environment as pathological. I agree with the idea of suffering which is embedded in the definition that describes pathology, particularly as it relates to children who are dependent on adults, but do not have adults to nurture, guide and lead them toward independence. All students in America's schools - urban, rural, suburban, public or parochial - inherit values, attitudes, and behaviors from institutional traditions. Thus, many students in urban schools inherit unproductive traditions that inhibit their progress toward a successful future. I believe, therefore, strategic practices must be advanced to create new traditions for students—ones which will enable them to have the confidence to exchange the old ones for the new, especially in school.

Positive reinforcement is essential to helping students acquire new behaviors in school. Aubrey Daniels, author of *Bringing Out the Best in People*, states that we bring out the best in people by reinforcing the behaviors we want to occur. I believe that we create new traditions in schools by bringing to center stage before all students acceptable behaviors. New trends are the beginning stage of new traditions. Trends are intentionally guided behaviors, but traditions are those behaviors that seemingly emerge once behaviors, attitudes, and values become routine and eventually entrenched. Thus, incentives, encouragement, modeling and strict guidance must be used to foster an environment for new traditions to emerge in a schoolhouse.

As stated already, positive reinforcement of a behavior is key to ensuring the behavior happens again. Therefore, attractive incentives must be used with students when creating a new trend of behaviors. It is important for the staff to pinpoint the behavior that is expected. However, possessing positively reinforcing models of good behavior in front of their peers will also encourage new behaviors that ultimately create a new tradition. Finally, the shaping of behaviors requires strict disciplinary procedures using negative reinforcement, penalty, and punishment as required.

Behaviors are not changed overnight. Students who are not accustomed to structure and have only experienced an unstructured environment, where a balance of love and discipline has not been used to reinforce behavior, will find it difficult to exist within a school environment where rules and respect for authority are the order of the day. Disruptive behavior that breaches school rules is plain evidence that structure causes pain for many students. Adults, however, must stay the course in enforcing the rules. Negative reinforcements (taking away something), penalty (losing something you have), and punishment (getting something that you don't want) are essential to creating new trends in student behaviors. Once firmly established, adults must interact with students consistently so that student behavior becomes automatic.

IMPORTANCE OF ACTION RESEARCH

Any urban administrator would benefit greatly by qualitative and quantitative research skills along with *good ol' heartfelt will* on the job. Action research skills help the leader manage change, plan and make adjustments in the midst of it. Principals who are action researchers are always defining the problem. Qualitative research skills are invaluable for an urban administrator because the problems faced are enormous, and they seemingly occur frequently and simultaneously.

An educational asset for principals who have action research skill is their ability to understand students' and parents' issues from their vantage point. Kenneth Pike discusses the term "emic" to mean the point of view understood from the actor's versus the observer's perspective. To establish an accurate emic point of view, the principal must observe, ask questions, and verify his conclusions about his students through them. Principals, however, who have an emic understanding of the behaviors and attitudes students bring to the school will be able to bring the sensitivity to the programming and planning processes designed to assist students.   Thus, action research skills are assets that will contribute greatly to the urban administrator's repertoire.

THE PRINCIPAL'S PARENTAL POWER

In a law class that I was enrolled in years ago, I was introduced to the Latin term *In Loco Parentis*. The English translation means in place or role of the parent. This term defines the legal authority given to responsible citizens to petition on the behalf of students. The principal is empowered with this authority for 180 days per year, seven hours per day and for as many students who enter the school daily.

As a principal working in an urban school system, serving as the parent on location is inescapable if you care about children. The image that caring principals establish makes it almost impossible not to get involved in student matters as a parent figure. The drug epidemic and its rippling affect alone, in many cities, pushes children to stressful circumstances that ultimately affect their performance in school. Thus, a caring principal finds himself intervening to try to help mitigate the pressure students are feeling.

The position of principal brings with it the notion of authority. Therefore, a principal who is an effective disciplinarian can help shape the lives of many students.

Another critical attribute for principals is flexibility. Flexibility includes a balance of disciplining and caring for students. Both discipline and care by the administrator involve limits in which students are given to operate. Students are told what to expect given certain behavior, and it is important for the administrator to follow through according to what she articulated to the students. Remember, consequences are both pleasant and unpleasant. Thus, students who demonstrate the appropriate behavior should be given consequences accordingly. Conversely, those demonstrating inappropriate behaviors should receive consequences accordingly.

Finally, the principal can also serve as the motivator for students. Students seem to enjoy when that "busy" man or lady takes time to center with them and encourage them relative to issues that are of concern to them. The principal is quite noticeable from where he sits. The students more than others know he is there. The power principals have to persuade, encourage, and shape students' lives, similar to that of parents, is tremendous. Therefore, *In Loco Parentis,* powers should be used wisely.

DUPLICATING LEADERSHIP

After reading a number of articles and books about the qualities of effective principals, as well as talking with such colleagues as Sarah Horsey, a Principal in the Edison Project, Mariale Hardiman, Principal of Roland Park Middle School, Frank Whorley former Principal of Mt. Royal Middle School, and Wyatt Coger former Principal of Harlem Park Middle School, several attributes consistently emerged in our conversation as those that are essential to have if one is going to be an effective leader in an urban school. Talking with these leaders, I discovered that principals' leadership qualities are divided into two categories: leadership and management. The former category is the essence of the principalship. Management, on the other hand, entails being clear about who will do what job and then reminding one's self to follow-up on the effectiveness of those individuals in their jobs.

Essential leadership qualities are paramount if the goals in the school organization are going to be achieved. The principal should be a *verbal inspirer* and *motivator*. She should articulate and keep the vision and goals of the school before the staff and students. The principal must have self-confidence. She acts only after reflecting on and testing the strategies and activities to be implemented. Students and staff should see a principal who is fair, firm, and consistent in her actions. Being optimistic and seeing the good and value in people are also qualities of a good Principal. She must be energetic while moving around the building to connect with staff and students. Knowing the culture and the realities of the students is also an important quality of the principal.

Finally, the principal must be sensitive to students and staff and care about them professionally. These attributes serve as indicators principals can use to do self-reflection. To find leaders who will commit to these qualities is to find principals who will be School Impact Leaders. Occasionally, principals' self-perceptions are skewed. In other words, we might think we are successful at certain tasks when in fact we really are not. Therefore, it is important that we remain open and approachable as leaders. This posture as a leader will allow us to get the "real deal" relative to the perceptions of those we lead. I believe that redundancy breeds reliability. In other words, if the same perception about one's leadership style continues to arise, there is a strong possibility there is some validity regarding the same. One of my colleagues used to say, *"A thousand Africans can't be wrong."*

Finally, principals can increase their effectiveness by acquiring thinking habits which help them respond to recurring situations. I have established eleven principles that consistently guide my thinking in the leadership process:

BUNDLEY'S TOP 10 LEADERSHIP MAXIMS

1. Its not where you live, but where and what you give.

Often, many are heard justifying why they don't participate in causes or movements that are not in proximity to where they reside even when it is clear that the purpose of such movements is worthy of their endorsement. I encourage those of this thinking to renew their minds considering the preceding maxim.

Remember, wherever you are, you can make a difference and a contribution to a worthy cause.

2. Listen to individuals' creeds, but watch for their deeds.

It is not what individuals' say but what they ultimately do that makes a difference.

3. Godly "deception" is a necessity to gain favor.

Deception is usually associated with something evil or fiendish. To leaders I say there are times for craftiness to be used to effectively win the minds and hearts of individuals in order to positively direct them. In 1 Corinthians, chapter 8, verses 19-22, it is stated best:

> "For though I am free from all men, I have made myself a servant to all, that I might win the more; and to the Jews I became as a Jew, that I might win the Jews; to those who are under the law, as under the law, that I might win those who are under the law; to those who are without law, as without law (not being without law toward God, but under the law toward Christ), that I may win those who are without law; to the weak I became as weak, that I might win the weak. I have become all things to all men that I might save some."

Centering, i.e. becoming a part of those you lead is essential.

4. Always ask yourself: What is the polarity of this idea being presented?

Every idea has its extreme. It should be standard practice for leaders to calculate the extreme of any idea presented. To realize the opposite is to have a necessary scope of a concept. Thus, as a leader, one will be better positioned to make an informed choice.

5. Skepticism is healthy.

To arbitrarily believe every idea presented to you can be detrimental to your mental health. Incredulity is a sign of psychological balance in the leader.

6. Know the difference between matters of the heart and matters of the head.

People closest to the leader have a tendency to enter the leader's psychological and emotional cavities more deeply than casual acquaintances and cohorts. The penetrative depth by love ones into the heart of the leader is achieved because of the emotional bonds established. It is natural; however, the leader should recognize the effect of these bonds. Then, mental strategies can be used to avoid being emotionally disabled. Thus, it will only remain for the leader to interact, mentally, with those who do not have the influence to take an emotional toll.

7. Seek individuals' common issues of interest and help them create a workable plan of action.

Individuals in organizations are usually influenced by common systems. These systems, in many instances, pose similar opportunities and obstacles. It is especially in the leaders' best interests to know what particular burdens or barriers are collectively perceived by professionals in the organization and openly participate in helping to alleviate or remove them.

8. Identify pockets of power, seize them and act strategically to leverage it appropriately.

Energy and force are synonyms for power. Force influences the direction in which people in organizations move. Leaders must ensure that the direction in which those in the organization is moving is confluent with the mission and vision. When this is not the case, the leader must position the fulcrum precisely to leverage power for the benefit of the organization.

9. Always diligently strive to be all God expects.

Everyone has a purpose. To actualize our purpose, we have been given gifts and talents. We must strive with these gifts and talents to be all we can be.

10. Massive momentum creates an image that influences people.

People engage and participate in causes which capture their attention and sponsor their latent desires.

Enough said! Let it be so!

HOME, COMMUNITY AND RELIGIOUS ORGANIZATION SUPPORT

There was an article in a local newspaper where the author concluded that school improvement in urban America will be far-fetched if there is not concerted effort by government, business, and community leaders to help transform the communities from which the school children come. Nothing could be closer to this truth. As I stated in the introduction of this book, to be an urban educator is to do the job given all of the issues brought to the school from the community and there are plenty.

Principals who choose to work in urban America choose to provide leadership that will make a positive impact despite the dislocation in all urban school districts. Thus, a plan to progress must be created regardless of the odds. In order to relocate and reconnect students to the educational process, there must be community involvement. In many urban communities one cannot help but notice the predominant number of churches and mosques.

I believe that the community leadership, if they would only act in a unified manner, could positively in influence the lives of students and consequently encourage them to do well in school. Everyday, young people pass by scores of store-front churches, modest sanctuaries, great mosques, colossal temples - all encumbered by an uneasiness with the plight of an underdeveloped city; uneasy with their idleness and the neglect of a desolate cry for divine intervention.

Worse even, many of our young people are members of these reverent halls of worship. At least once a Sunday, the young ladies drape themselves in cool cotton whites; the young men come with their upper most button on their collars buttoned. They are reminded of their burgeoning beauty and of their maturing strength. The pastor, minister, and priest all smile making such pleasantries, as they mark the seventy-five-cent tithe laced with hurried blessings. And on Monday through Saturday, the budding beauties and ripening boys are lost from memory. With some hope, they are regarded amidst some long night prayer inundated with supplication for health, healing, deliverance, and repentance. But with relentless effort, principals can connect with the religious leaders and have considerable effect on children, families, and the community at large.

Students' attitudes toward the school and school personnel change when they (students) believe that there is a connection between their community and the school. The church and mosques serve as a spiritual inspiration to many members (parents and students). Spiritual leaders can come to the school and participate in programs to demonstrate to students that they care. When students realize that the school personnel are familiar with those they respect and admire, their attitudes usually become more positive toward the school. Members of churches and mosques can also help create parent training programs. Such programs will also have a positive effect on students.

Recreation and youth centers are also prevalent in many urban communities. Usually, elementary and middle age students participate in activities at recreation and youth centers. School officials and youth center employees can devise a program that connects what students do in school to activities held in the youth centers. For example, students who participate in sports can be required to meet an academic standard in school. Funds can even be redirected in city government to have tutors placed in the recreation centers to help students with their studies before they participate in sports.

THE LAST HOPE FOR URBAN EDUCATION

Dr. Rudy Crew, former Superintendent for New York Public Schools asks, "The real issue for Urban America [regarding public school] is, can you replicate it [effective schools], can you do it in a cost effective way and can you create the organizational culture that gives rise to it on a scale that impacts the lives of every child in the system?"

I found Dr. Crew's questions to be both profound and concise. Accordingly, the answer to the question, I believe, will render information that will give urban educators a strong response and sound solution that for many brings a ray of hope relative to the effective longevity of urban education. The profundity of Dr. Crew's questions relate to replicating or "scaling up" effective school programs and recreating an organizational culture that ensures that ideas become a reality that impacts the lives of every child in a school system.

In order to replicate effective school programs and ensure that they reach all students, superintendents must move swiftly to select assistant superintendents who will help principals establish school improvement plans which will achieve immediate results—qualitative and quantitative alike. The adults in urban schools have the capacity not only to resuscitate the school systems, but restore healthy school programs that will give those who matriculate some options for their future.

There is a need for more money—no question. The superintendent must corral the troops who will fight on this front. However, effective principals leading teachers must be the focus in all school systems in urban America. Many give lip service to the idea of *Site Based Management*, but few engage principals around a collective focus, supporting them in the efforts to improve schools. This, however, must be the focus. I call this *In the Meantime Leadership*. In other words, until such time as schools are appropriately funded, we will teach; until such time we find and hire all certified teachers, we will lead; until such time parents of students stop subjecting children to undue stress because of their drug addiction, we will lead and teach. I can go on and on, but I won't.

In the meantime…nevertheless…we will do whatever it takes to educate America's children in urban America. I encourage you to take the ideas from this chapter and do what positive things you will.

* * * * * * * * *

"My people are destroyed for their lack of knowledge…"
Hosea 4:6

LIKE MINDS AND SPIRITS

CHAPTER NINE

Regarding African American students in predominantly white schools, I am greatly pained to read the newspaper and discover that parents of African American students from predominantly working class and productive families are allowing their children to perform at mediocre or worse academic levels. The energies that these parents must exert to make ends meet indicate to some degree their "like minds and spirits."

The lack of collective thought and motivation to demand academic excellence from their students and the school indicates misplaced priorities and divided thinking as a group. Given that all the elements for academic success are present, yet there are only bleak signs of success showing, forces me to conclude that the community of adults has shunned the need for Like Minds and Spirits to effectively address the academic underachievement of their children.

Fundamental to effectively addressing students' under performance is an agenda that addresses the real issues contributing to students' academic mediocrity. Remember! All elements needed for academic excellence – working parents, capable children, and educated teachers – are present. Thus, the looming question is: why do we not see academic excellence? To answer the question, I contend that curriculum issues are being ignored and methodologies that need to be implemented are not.

While in graduate school at Penn State University, I came to understand the idea of curriculum to be a course of study pursued to obtain information to be used to achieve specific learning goals. Where students are *not* achieving, especially when they have the wherewithal to do so, concerned adults need to ferret out why such is the case. A curriculum process called "mapping" can be used to pinpoint issues contributing to student underachievement.

Within the curriculum mapping process, problems that students demonstrate or encounter are diagnosed. Once problems are identified and prescriptions are established by mapping the root cause of problems, then an appropriate remedy can be created. An appropriate remedy in a situation where African American students are underachieving when evidence clearly indicates they should be achieving must involve "truth telling" and "reality facing." William Jenkins, for example, contends in his book *Understanding and Educating African American Children* that there are factors that hinder Black children's performance in predominantly white schools.

More specifically, William Jenkins states, "white schools are not serving the needs of Black children because they are incompatible with the Black child and the Black community, and they lack knowledge, courage, and leadership to courageously address the issues that need addressing in the education of Black children." Mr. Jenkins further goes on to state factors that support the assertion above, which in the interest of time, I will not elaborate on.

However, as we get back to the curriculum mapping method as a process to be used to search out reasons for students' academic underachievement, I, like William Jenkins, believe that parents and community members must have the knowledge, courage, and leadership to insist that students who should demonstrate academic excellence do so.

When all indicators show that students should be performing, parents and concerned community members should assert facts in a logical manner so that they can prepare themselves to effectively act based upon the information derived from conclusions. For example, the syllogism below should be used by parents and community members who know their students should be performing, excellently:

> - My child is capable of academic excellence.
> - His individual test scores and the collective test scores of his peers indicate academic mediocrity.
> ___
> - Therefore, there are specific factors stopping my child from performing excellently.

Now, I must say here as Dr. Tyrone Powers would say, "There is a burden and beauty to knowledge." The knowledge that parents and community members glean from the conclusion after logical examination of the problem of student underachievement puts them in a position of accountability. Thus, the burden of knowing students should be achieving academically when they are not should cause concerned individuals to examine themselves first, by asking how or did I contribute to the situation before me? This crucial question opens the flood gate for truth to enter.

I have learned that truth has a way of making one react receptively or rejectively. Receptive behavior on the part of parents will spur them to create corrective action regarding the problem of student underachievement in school. On the other hand, rejective behavior will manifest parents and community members placing the responsibility of student academic achievement at the foot of the school's steps assuming that school officials will take full responsibility for educating the students and to educate students appropriately even with the consistent absence of parents and community members in the school.

Not only will the truth impel one to own or shun responsibility for low academic achievement, those who own the circumstance incur a further burden just for their stance, however unpopular, to redress student lack of academic achievement. Actually, the action that concerned adults take is the beginning of the added burden. The actions necessary to correct student underachievement are a consistent occupation, often with few breaks on the way to a remedy.

William Jenkins cites several adjustments needed if Black students are to do well in predominantly white schools. Here, I share five of his citations. He states generally that adjustments must be made with:

- Professional staff that is white and/or middle class Black that does not relate to the life styles and values of children…

- A refusal to study Black cultural influences as a legitimate social phenomenon that shapes Black people…

- A political and school climate that would rather have peace than address tough issues in the education of Black children…

- Too few black faculty to serve as mentors and leaders for Black children…

- The acceptance of black academic mediocrity and social incorrigibility as normal.

Effective action to address the issues asserted by William Jenkins clearly requires dialogue between those concerned. Resolutions of the issue will not come without concentrated effort and energy. A parallel experience will be encountered by parents and concerned community members who collectively mobilize to address the academic under achievement of their students. These individuals must bring their concerns and educational strategies to the schoolhouse and work in concert with school officials to create strategies that produce academic excellence.

The burden of knowledge is eventually hoisted by individuals or groups sustained by work and responsibility to correct or attain established goals which come into focus because of enlightenment. Thus, enlightenment is the beauty of knowledge that fosters momentum. Parents and community members who have implemented strategies to increase their children's academic achievement gain more confidence and ownership in the endeavor when they observe the "fruits of their labor." Thus, future educational issues concerning their students become naturally theirs to address with Like Minds and Spirits.

Finally, Drs. Nathan and Julia Hare state that the centrifugal work which comes from school officials is important in the development of students, but the centripetal work of parents and concerned community members is absolutely essential. Urban education will only become effective when the seemingly difficult task of getting those in the communities surrounding the school to act collectively to help and support children.

PYRAMID OF EDUCATIONAL INTERVENTION

Urban education is perceived to be in crisis across this nation. Those in power share this perception after they examine student achievement data and realize that urban students are underachieving on non-standardized and standardized academic measures. Lately, it has been politically acceptable and correct for educators and leaders of urban school reform to rush quickly to for-profit companies and non-profit foundations to solicit expertise and help in order to curb the failure rates of school districts. There seems to be some benefit and academic success for students whose schools have been turned over to for-profit companies and educational foundations. However, the real answer for failing urban schools rests deep inside the people of the communities from which the students come. This answer comes in the form of commitment, vision, leadership and will. These attributes are essential for urban educators who stay the course in the midst of political, economic, and social inequities.

Recently, I pondered what is different between the "old" failing public schools and the "new" for-profit/foundation-run schools from which services have been solicited by policy makers of various school districts. My reflections rendered the following thoughts about the "new" schools. "New" school leaders:

- Select personnel with a streamlined and collective focus.
- Enjoy district level support.
- Receive increased financial resources.

When I think about the amenities listed which leaders of "new" schools have at their disposal to help them effectuate the running of their school, I can only conclude that all schools could be effective with the will and support from district level leaders and committed politicians. Unfortunately, district level policy makers and politicians, alone, are seldom the combination needed to expedite the distribution of educational resources (i.e. financial and material) for the urban child.

Furthermore, there is such a fickle nature that resides in policymakers and politicians in leadership positions. In order to equitably allocate resources, there needs to be caring and committed constituents from the community who strategically make demands from policymakers and politicians alike, while making community education a focus that pervades every area. Community education entails, first, citizens from the neighborhoods addressing all conditions that prevent them from being physically, emotionally, socially, and spiritually whole. There has to be a movement by the citizenry to primarily solve their own problems and promote their own development. Remember! The school can improve no more than the community, because they are one in the same.

Communities' self-determination and collective consciousness are the only answers to sustained educational improvement in urban America. If one looks at the amenities imbedded in these ideas, while they might not be exhaustive, they are clearly evident in newly established for-profit and foundation-run schools. It occurred to me while thinking about what "new" schools enjoy that all schools should have the same. The resources given to these new schools really should be the minimum expectations for all urban schools. By the way, I am discussing the education of our children in urban America. Or are these, for the most part, black, brown, red and poor white children significant enough targets to be included on society's educational radar screen? The answer for me is yes. But how many leaders will stand with me in deed, not mere creed, and agree?

While this community movement to improve education is gaining momentum, committed educators and administrators must establish a pyramid of educational intervention strategies that will help them demand the best of students while they are in school. Below I describe the pyramid of intervention used at the high school where I served as principal. These intervention strategies were established with the following thought in mind: Give every student an opportunity to succeed in school.

EPILOGUE

We deemed it important to address student truancy so we partnered with the juvenile court system to inform truant students and their parents about the importance of school attendance and the unfortunate consequences when students did not consistently attend school. An in-school adjustment center was essential for students who misbehaved and warranted a consequence, but did not need to be sent home. Students would be sent to the adjustment center inside the school to serve out the consequence for their misbehavior.

Another intervention that gave students an opportunity to succeed was a Credit Recovery Program. This program allowed students to repeat courses failed. However, the repeated courses are studied on Saturday and in the evening. Finally, the Student Support Team (SST), which is mandated policy for the school system, is a collective planning process by adult staff to ensure that students' academic needs are monitored during the school year.

A pyramid of intervention for students is a natural fit for me in the administrative process. It is extremely important that students in the urban setting are given a second and sometimes a third chance to achieve educational excellence. Often, many of these students experience difficulties that others can only imagine. I speak here from experience. Malcolm X taught that *will* allows an individual an opportunity to succeed if he/she uses time wisely. This idea must be encouraged in our students.

BIBLIOGRAPHY

Akbar, N. (1985). The community of self (revised). Florida: Mind Productions & Associates.

Akbar, N. (1998). Know thy self. Florida: Mind Productions.

Belasco, J. (1991). Teaching the elephant to dance: the manager's guide to empowering change. New York: Plume {Penguin Group}.

Belasco, J., and Ralph Stayer (1993). Flight of the buffalo: soaring to excellence, learning to let employees lead. New York: Warner.

Boldt, L. (1996). How to find the work you love. New York: Penguin.

Covey, S. (1989). The 7 habits of highly effective people: powerful lessons in personal change. New York: Simon & Schuster.

Daniels, A. (1990). Bringing out the best in people. New York: McGraw Hill.

Davis, G. & Margaret Thomas. (1989). Effective schools and effective teachers. Boston, Massachusetts: Allyn and Bacon.

Friere, P. (1970). Pedagogy of the oppressed. New York: Continuum.

Frank, L.R. Quotationary (1999). New York: Random House.

Garbarino, J. (1999). Lost Boys: Why our sons turn violent and how we can save them. New York: The Free Press.

Garvey, A. (1986). The philosophy & opinions of marcus garvey or, africa for the africans. Massachusetts: The Majority Press. {New Preface-Tony Martin}

Gauld, J. (1933). Character first: the hyde school difference. San Francisco, California: ICS {Institute of Comtemporary Studies} PRESS.

Glasser, W.(1990). The quality school: managing students without coercion. New York: Harper Perennial.

Glasser, W. (1985). Control theory in the classroom. New York: Harper & Row.

BIBLIOGRAPHY

Glasser, W. (1965). Reality therapy: a new approach to psychiatry. New York: Harper & Row.

Sullivan, G & Harper, M. (1996). Hope is not a method: what business leaders can learn from americans army. New York: Random House.

Hare, N (1991). The hare plan: to overhaul the public schools and educate every black man, woman and child. San Francisco, California: The Black Think Tank.

Howard, J. (1992). Napolean Hill: think and grow rich. Efficacy Institute.

Hrabowski III, F., Maton, Kenneth., Geoffrey Greif (1998). Beating the odds: raising academically successful african america males. New York: Oxford University Press.

Hubbard, E. (1923). Elbert Hubbard's Scrap Book. New York: Roycrofters.

Jenkins, W. (1990). Understanding and educating african american children. San Louis, Missouri: William Jenkins Enterprise

BIBLIOGRAPHY

Kouzes, J., Barry Posner (1993). Credibility: how leaders gain and lose it, why people demand it. San Francisco, California: Jossey-Bass Publishers.{Forward-Tom Peters}

Krzyzewski, M. w/ Donald T. Phillips (2000). Leading with the heart: coach k's successful strategies for basketball, business, and life. New York: Warner Books.

Manske, F. (1990). Secrets of effective leadership: A practical guide to success. Columbia, TN: Leadership education and Development, Inc.

Maxwell, J. (1998). The 21 irrefutable laws of leadership: follow them and people will follow you. Tennessee: Thomas Nelson Publishers.

Mfume, K. (1997). No free ride: from mean streets to mainstream. One World/Ballantine. Canada.

Mosle, S. (August, 1997). The stealth chancellor. The New York Times Magazine. Section 6.

Munroe, M. (1993). Becoming a leader: everyone can do it. California: Pneuma Life Publishing.

BIBLIOGRAPHY

NASSP. (1996). Breaking Ranks: Changing an American Institution. Western Virginia.

Payne, R. (1998). A framework for understanding poverty. Texas: R.F.T Publishing Co.

Pike,K.(1954). Language in relation to a unified theory of the structure of human behavior. Vol 1. Glendale, California: Summer Institute of Linguistics.

Reid III, F. (1993). The nehemiah plan: preparing the church to rebuild broken lives. Pennsylvania: Treasure House.

Robbins, A.(1986). Unlimited power. New York: Fawcett Columbine.

Robbins, A. & McClendon III, J.(1997). The unlimited power: a black choice. New York: Simon & Schuster.

Roger-John & McWilliams, P. (1991). Do It! Let's get off our buts. Los Angelos, California: Prelude Press.

Senge, P.(1990). The fifth discipline: The art & practice of the learning organization. New York: Doubleday.

BIBLIOGRAPHY

Senge, P.; Ross, R.; Smith, B.; Roberts, C.; Kleiner, A.(1994). The Fifth Discipline Fieldbook: strategies and tools for building a learning organization. New York: Doubleday

T' Shaka, O. (1990). The art of leadership. Vol. I. California: Pan Afrikan Publications.

Waitley, D. (1995). Empires of the mind: lessons to lead and succeed in a knowledge-based world. New York: Willliam Morrow and Company, Inc.

Waitley, D. (1983). Seeds of greatness: The ten best-kept secrets of total success. New York: Pocket Books.

Williams, T. (1994). The personal touch: what you really need to succeed in today's fast-paced business world. New York: Warner Books. {w/Joe Cooney; forward by Bill Cosby}

Woodson, C. (1933). Mis-education of the negro. Washington, D.C.: The Associated Publishers, Inc. {Edited and Intro by Charles Wesley and Thelma D. Perry}

* * * * * * * * * *

Dr. Andrey L. Bundley

Andrey Bundley was raised in Baltimore, Maryland and educated in the Baltimore City Public School System. He earned a Bachelor of Science degree from Coppin State University, a Masters of Education Degree in Counselor Education, and a Doctorate in Curriculum and Instruction from Penn State University. Dr. Bundley began his teaching career at Harlem Park Middle School in 1985 and thereafter accepted the position of Educational Consultant at Penn State University. Dr. Bundley returned to Baltimore in 1990 as a professor at Coppin State University. In 1992, he served as an Assistant Principal at Thurgood Marshall Middle School in Prince Georges County and at Harlem Park Middle School in Baltimore before he was promoted to Principal of Greenspring Middle School. During his three year tenure at Greenspring, Dr. Bundley was the youngest principal in the state of Maryland. Currently Dr. Bundley serves as the principal of Walbrook High School Uniform Services Academy. He is also a role model for many African American youth as well as a highly sought after motivational speaker and educational consultant. Dr. Bundley is married to his sweetheart, Shelia, and they are the proud parents of their son, Dreyan.

* * * * * * * * * *

Deborah
Bailey
—